DINNER
· FOR DOGS ·

To my family
Kim, Holly and Lily

DINNER
· FOR DOGS ·

· HOME COOKING FOR A HAPPY, HEALTHY DOG ·

HENRIETTA MORRISON
OF LILY'S KITCHEN

EBURY
PRESS

1 3 5 7 9 10 8 6 4 2

Published in 2012 by Ebury Press, an imprint of Ebury Publishing
A Random House Group Company
Text © Henrietta Morrison 2012
Cover and p. 8 photograph copyright © Vicki Couchman 2012

The Random House Group Limited Reg. No. 954009
Addresses for companies within the Random House Group can be found at
www.randomhouse.co.uk

A CIP catalogue record for this book is available from the British Library

The Random House Group Limited supports The Forest Stewardship Council (FSC®), the
leading international forest certification organisation. Our books carrying the FSC label are
printed on FSC® certified paper. FSC is the only forest certification scheme endorsed by the
leading environmental organisations, including Greenpeace. Our paper procurement policy can
be found at www.randomhouse.co.uk/environment

To buy books by your favourite authors and register for offers visit www.randomhouse.co.uk

Project editor: Anne McDowall
Design and illustrations: Mad River

Printed and bound in China by Toppan Leefung

ISBN 9780091947071

Note: The information in this book has been compiled by way of general guidance in relation to cooking for dogs.
It is not a substitute and not to be relied on for specific nutritional, dietary or other professional advice on specific
circumstances and in specific locations. Please consult your dog's veterinary advisor before changing, stopping or
starting any medical or other treatment relating to your dog. So far as the author is aware the information given is
correct and up to date as at February 2012. Practice, laws and regulations all change, and the reader should obtain up
to date professional advice on any such issues. The author and publishers disclaim, as far as the law allows, any liability
arising directly or indirectly from the use, or misuse, of the information contained in this book.

Contents

The only question in life that really matters to dogs is: 'What's for dinner?'! As pet owners, we feel a deep-down satisfaction when we see our dogs tucking into their food. Luckily, feeding time in our house is a moment of much excitement and anticipation.

If your dog goes off his or her food, it's usually a sign that something's up. I know how concerning this can be: when my dog Lily was a year old, she stopped eating altogether. She would run up to her bowl with her usual exuberance and then back away slowly. I was horrified! I tried different foods, but to no avail; she would seem enthusiastic until she smelt what was in the bowl and would then turn away and wander off looking rather dejected. I started cooking her some chicken, rice, vegetables and apples, which I knew she loved, and she began to eat properly again. This was definitely good news all round and I kept a copy of the recipes I made.

Cooking for your pet is easy, satisfying and a great way to bond! It is good to know that what you have prepared is a nourishing, yummy meal that is real food and not the grease-laden dry pellets or chunk-and-jelly that are generally sold in shops.

LILY

Healthy eating for dogs

The philosophy behind each recipe in this book is Hippocrates' holistic mantra 'Let Food Be Thy Medicine and Medicine Thy Food'. Eating well will contribute to your good health and eating badly will be detrimental, and the same goes for our pets. If it's not good enough for me, it's not good enough for Lily. That's not to say Lily should eat what I eat (too many croissants would be on the list!), but if I'm not prepared to eat it, then I don't feed it to my dog.

Ready-made versus home-cooked

Providing food for your dog is your responsibility as a pet owner. There are several ways of doing this: you can roll up your sleeves and get cooking, buy a really good ready-made food, or try a combination of both.

It's always been a tricky thing to know what to feed your dog. There's a pretty assertive lobby from pet food manufacturers who warn you not to cook for your pet under any circumstances because you may not be feeding them properly or, worse, may be making them ill.

I think there needs to be a clear distinction between cooking for your pet, which is an extremely rewarding and caring thing to do, and giving your pet leftover scraps of pizza, curries and the like, which have little nutritional value to your dog.

It's also good to give your dog a varied diet so they benefit from the whole spectrum of nutrients. You'll find more on the 'building blocks' of a healthy diet for your pet on pages 12–23.

> **If it's not good enough for me, it's not good enough for Lily. ... if I'm not prepared to eat it, then I don't feed it to my dog.**

Raw Food

I often get asked about raw food. I'm not an advocate, as I'm concerned about the parasites in raw food and the stories I hear of how raw food has made some dogs very ill. Raw food advocates put forward the argument that your dog is healthier and looks better on raw food. For me this is not the case – what is important is that you feed your dog good food. Whether it is cooked or not is not the point. Interestingly Harvard University recently published a study showing that cooking food for mammals makes it much more easy for them to digest and metabolize than raw food.

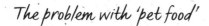

The problem with 'pet food'

Buying food for your pet has turned into a bit of a minefield. In around nine out of ten supermarkets, pet food will be on the same aisle as laundry products. This is because pet food has been viewed as a commodity just like washing powder. Supermarkets bulk buy at the cheapest prices, and it's a market that is almost solely controlled by huge multinationals that are experts at producing millions of tins of dog food an hour.

But for me, food for your dog should be just that – real food made from ingredients you or I would recognize immediately. One of the things that has amazed me is that we owners don't trust our instincts when we are buying food for our pets. Even though the food may smell awful and contain all sorts of horrible things, we still carry on buying it and feeding it to our dogs.

Cheap dog food is cheap for a reason: the only way it's possible to sell a huge bag of dog food for a few pounds is to make it using extremely low-grade, waste ingredients from the food industry – restaurant oils, tomato skins, twigs and pips from grapes, heat-blasted carcasees… The list goes on.

You'll find more information on how to read a dog food label to help you navigate your way through all the pet foods on the market on pages 24–7.

Using the recipes in this book

The recipes in this book are designed to be easy, healthy and low fat. There is no added salt and most of the recipes are wheat gluten free. You will find here a selection of everyday meals and treats, as well as recipes suitable for old dogs and those that have been unwell.

They do not claim to be complete meals as we would then have to get very technical about adding in enough calcium, making sure there's not too much copper, etc. Complete pet foods have a wide range of vitamins added to them to make sure they provide the full spectrum of nutrition. Your vet is the best person to talk to about nutrition for your particular dog.

I've included some nutritional information as a guide to what's in the recipe. These have been calculated on an 'as fed' basis – this means that you get the nutritional value of the cooked food. This will give you some guidelines on how calorific the recipes are and how much fat and protein they provide.

My advice would be to try to make the time to prepare a home-cooked meal for your dog at least once a week. If you have time for more, then great and if not, then make sure that on the other days you are feeding your dog a really good food. Don't go for the cheapest option; buy the best food you can – your dog is worth it!

Remember: our dogs depend on us solely for their food and nourishment – indeed for their survival. Lily is so excited to see me every morning! I know she loves me, but I also know she's excited as it means breakfast is on its way!

I hope you have fun cooking these delicious recipes from Lily's Kitchen.

Henrietta

Top Tip

Cooking for your dog is easy: it takes a bit more time than opening a tin, but you can make the food in batches and either refrigerate or freeze it.

The building blocks of a healthy diet

It is important if you are planning to cook for your dog on a fairly regular basis that you provide a balanced diet of proteins, fats and carbohydrates. Complete dog food contains all these elements as well as the necessary vitamins, amino acids and minerals, such as calcium, that are important to keep your dog in good health. It's also good to provide a variety of ingredients so that your dog gets the whole spectrum of nutrition available from a wide range of ingredients. I do rather feel sorry for the poor fellow who has to eat the same brand of dry kibble for ever. It would be a bit like us eating buttered toast for every meal for ever – it would keep us alive but wouldn't really keep us in peak health.

Proteins

Proteins are essential for your dog for good muscle and healthy tissue growth. Animal proteins – found in meat, fish, poultry, eggs and some dairy products – are the easiest for your dog to digest and make the best use of. Proteins from plant sources are harder to digest and do not contain the full range of essential amino acids that dogs need. However, you can combine different proteins together and include beans, peas and lentils for their protein content.

Meat is a rich source of protein, minerals and vitamins. It is, however, low in calcium and relatively high in phosphorus. If you are cooking for your dog regularly – let's say more than three times a week – you will need to add a calcium source such as raw meaty bones or fresh bone meal to his or her daily rations in order to ensure a healthy level of these two important minerals. Fatty meat is actually good for dogs: if they eat only lean meat, they will be missing out on some key vitamins (see opposite).

Remember to include organ meat too as this includes a critical array of nutrients not found in muscle meat. Liver and kidneys are a rich source of vitamins, especially vitamin A and minerals. The recipes here are made with a range of different meats, including chicken, turkey, fish, beef and lamb. Variety, as in all parts of a balanced diet, is the key, so try cooking different meats for your dog. Bland, white meat, such as chicken, is easier to digest and hence a good choice for a convalescent dog.

Feeding your dog twice a day rather than once makes it easier for him or her to digest food properly. And it means your dog will look forward to something twice a day rather than once – double happiness!

Fats – for energy

Dogs love the taste of fat, especially animal fat. You'll notice there's always a very willing eater of leftover fat from a juicy steak! Fats are a very important part of your pet's diet. Fats act as a carrier for the important fat-soluble vitamins, such as Vitamins A, D, E and K.

However, it's really important to strike a balance between feeding enough fat for good health, but not so much that your lovely lean dog turns into a bit of a heavyweight. An overweight dog is also prone to other serious health problems, such as pancreatitis. Per gram, fat contains twice as many calories as protein or carbohydrates.

Essential fatty acids play an important role and are essential to your dog's health. Dogs need to have these included in their diet as they cannot make them themselves. EFAs are crucial to every cell in your dog's body, and aid in the regulation of nearly every bodily function. They play a key role in helping to regulate the immune system and can act as powerful anti-inflammatories. They are also particularly important for maintaining a healthy skin and coat, for brain and kidney function and for a healthy heart. The most important families of fatty acids are the omega-3s and the omega-6s.

Omega-6 (also known as linoleic acid) is found in ingredients such as sunflower oil.

It plays an important role in skin health, tissue repair and in providing a healthy immune system. However, too much omega-6 can cause skin allergies and other problems. Most diets already contain enough omega-6, so concentrate on making sure your dog gets enough omega-3 fatty acids.

The richest sources of omega-3 are fish, particularly coldwater, oily fish such as salmon, herring, mackerel, anchovies and sardines, all of which are good to feed your dog. These are all full of docosahexaenoic acid (DHA) and eicosapentaenoic acid (EPA), which are the chemical names for the omega-3s. There is also a type of omega-3, alpha linolenic acid (ALA), that is found in plants, most importantly in flaxseed oil and hempseed oil. (This is why at Lily's Kitchen we add organic flaxseed oil to all our recipes.)

I wouldn't recommend giving your dog extra omega-3 or -6 supplements without discussing this with your vet first, as too much can cause a variety of health problems and suppress the immune system.

Although commonly given, cod liver oil is not a beneficial supplement for your dog. This is because it contains high levels of vitamins A and D, which if given daily can build up and cause toxicity. For cooking purposes, I generally use rapeseed oil or olive oil, which are more resistant to the damaging effects of heat than other vegetable oils. Try to stick to a rough guide of one tablespoon of oil for your dog per day — half this amount if you have a small dog.

> **EFAs are important for maintaining a healthy skin and coat, for brain and kidney function and for a healthy heart.**

Carbohydrates

These are very important as they supply the fuel for activity as well as being a source of fibre, which helps the gastro-intestine to function happily. Good sources of fibre include oats, brown rice, potato and whole wheats. Vegetables and fruit also provide carbohydrates. Grains are basic energy foods – they are a source of complex carbohydrates. Many commercial dog foods have a very high level of grains. Dogs benefit from having a low amount of grain in their diet – up to 30% is fine. By using a few well-selected whole grains in the recipes you cook, you will provide your dog with the benefits of slow-release energy (low GI), fibre and a wide range of important vitamins and minerals (notably vitamin E and B complex). In addition to providing energy, carbohydrates maintain the health of the thyroid, liver, heart, brain and nervous tissue.

On the following pages you will find an introduction to some of the cereal grains available for use in recipes for your dog; choose different ones for their particular qualities.

Buying & Cooking Grain

- Buy whole grains as they have greater nutritional benefits
- Always rinse grains well before use
- Soaking grains overnight before cooking helps to increase digestibility and nutritional value. (You can cook the grain in this nutrient rich water).

Introducing grains

Barley

This is the mildest and least irritating of all the cereals and therefore often used for feeding dogs that are unwell. Pearled barley has had the inedible outer hulls removed. Barley has low gluten content, a mild, sweet flavour and a pleasing, chewy texture. It helps to nourish and soothe the entire gastro-intestinal tract. Barley is highly nutritious and good for underweight dogs that need building up.

*gluten free

Buckwheat*

A power-packed grain, buckwheat is special in that it contains many essential amino acids as well as a substance called rutin that helps strengthen the capillaries and aids the circulation. It is an excellent grain for cold weather months because of the warming and drying effects on the body. It has a reputation of being a good blood builder and neutralizer of toxic wastes. This is a gluten-free grain with a sweet flavour. It cleanses the intestines and improves appetite.

Calcium

It is important when feeding dogs an entirely home-cooked diet to make sure there's enough calcium in their diet. Calcium's main sources are raw bones, dark green leafy vegetables, pulses, dairy products and egg shells.

Corn/Maize*

The most widely grown crop worldwide, with a large percentage now GM, corn can be used as a grain, an oil or a flour (corn flour). It is a gluten-free grain with a sweet flavour. However, although most commercial dog foods, particularly in the US, are made with a huge proportion of corn, many dogs do find corn quite hard to digest, so I haven't included corn or maize in any of the recipes in this book.

Millet*

Exceedingly nutritious, millet contains an abundance of minerals and vitamins and the most complete protein of any of the cereal grains. Millet is one of the least allergenic foods, so good for dogs with a sensitive digestion.

Oats

Great for maintaining energy and warmth during the cold winter months because they contain more fat and protein than most other grains, oats are an adaptogen grain, meaning that they improve the body's resistance to stress and help keep the system in a healthy state of balance. Oats support the nervous system and help regulate the thyroid gland. Like all whole grains, oats have a mild laxative action as they are high in fibre.

Quinoa*

Pronounced keen-wah, quinoa was a principle grain of the Incas, given sacred status as a 'mother grain'. Because it is energy and protein rich, quinoa is a particularly valuable grain to use for convalescing dogs, as well as for those that have a tendency to a sensitive digestion. Quinoa contains a balanced set of essential amino acids (it contains lysine, which is missing or low in many cereal grains), making it the most complete protein source among plant foods. It is also a good source of fibre and phosphorus and is high in magnesium and iron. In fact, quinoa is such a 'super-food' that it is being considered by NASA as a food for astronauts!

*gluten free

Rice

A staple grain for more than of half the world's population (the Chinese word for rice means 'grain of life'), rice is a sweet, neutral grain that is often recommended as part of the diet in convalescence because it helps to soothe the stomach and expel toxins from the system. Rice is said to calm the nervous system, relieve depression and strengthen the internal organs. Wholegrain rice is a source of B vitamins.

Rye

Closely related to barley and wheat but with a lower gluten content, rye has a strong flavour and is a versatile grain that can be combined with others. Rye is said to build strong muscles and promote energy and endurance. It benefits the liver and is said to aid nail, fur and bone formation. It is a filling grain and is high in soluble fibre.

Spelt

Believed to be among the most ancient of cultivated cereals, this type of wheat was highly favoured by the Romans. Spelt has a very low allergenic profile, so is ideally suited to dogs that are intolerant to gluten. At Lily's Kitchen we are the only pet food manufacturer to use spelt in our recipes. Its high water solubility makes spelt very easily absorbed in the body and hence easily digested. Because it is not a hybridized grain like wheat, it is generally higher in protein, vitamins and minerals.

Wheat

Wheat is said to have a calming effect on the mind. Wheat allergy may be linked to the huge quantity that is eaten, as well as to the highly refined state it is now in, since few individuals have allergies to the heirloom varieties of wheat such as kamut and spelt. Whole wheat is the most nutritious form of wheat; refined wheat has lost as much as 80 per cent of its vitamins and minerals and 93 per cent of its fibre. Wheat bran (the outer fibrous layers of the grain) is typically added to provide bulk and fibre to the diet and so is good for treating constipation. Wheat germ is nutritionally the best part and contains the entire vitamin B complex.

· Gluten Intolerance ·

Just as many people are gluten intolerant, so are a growing number of dogs. Gluten is a combination of two proteins found in many grains, but highest in wheat. (Gluten is what allows bread to rise – when the dough is kneaded, gluten traps the carbon dioxide released by the yeast.) The following grains are gluten free: amaranth, corn, millet, quinoa, rice and spelt (although the latter does contain gluten, sensitivity to spelt is very unusual).

Vegetables

About 20–30 per cent of your dog's diet should consist of fresh vegetables. Lightly steaming or cooking them makes them easier to digest. In addition to being full of antioxidants and other phytonutrients, vegetables are an important source of minerals, vitamins and fibre in the diet.

The following are all good vegetables to feed your dog:

Broccoli

A good summer vegetable that brightens the eyes and is helpful for eye inflammation, broccoli contains abundant pantothenic acid and vitamin A, which benefit rough skin. It contains more vitamin C than citrus fruits and is a high natural source of sulphur, iron and B vitamins. (Avoid in cases of thyroid deficiency.)

Butternut squash

Compared with summer squash, winter squash contains greater amounts of natural sugars, carbohydrates and vitamin A. Butternut squash has anti-inflammatory properties and is said to help get rid of intestinal parasites such as worms.

Cabbage

Green and purple cabbage improves digestion and circulation and is good for treating constipation. Cabbage contains iodine and is a rich source of vitamin C (it contains more than oranges). Vitamin E is concentrated in the outer leaves, which also contain at least a third more calcium than the inner ones.

Carrot

Carrots contain one of the richest sources of the anti-oxidant beta-carotene (provitamin A), which is said to protect against cancer. Beta-carotene/vitamin A benefits the skin and is anti-inflammatory for the intestinal lining.

• Top Tips •

- Wash vegetables before using them
- Steam or only lightly cook them – too much cooking destroys the goodness
- Add the cooking water to the food
- Include vegetables of a variety of colours, as they contain different phytonutrients and antioxidants
- If using raw vegetables, then purée or liquidize them before use
- Use vegetables that are in season.

Lentils

Lentils are a good source of soluble, digestible protein. They have diuretic action and are beneficial to the heart and circulation. They stimulate the adrenal system and increase the vitality of the kidneys.

Parsnips

Even richer in vitamins and minerals than carrots, parsnips are rich in potassium, and a great source of good-quality dietary fibre.

Peas

Peas harmonize digestion and are also diuretic and mildly laxative (so good for treating constipation) and used to counteract spasms.

Spinach

Likewise, spinach has diuretic action and a laxative effect. The rich iron and chlorophyll content of spinach builds blood. It also contains high levels of vitamin A.

Fruit

Fruit contains valuable minerals, vitamins, enzymes and fibre, and is easily digested. The alkaline element in fruit combined with its acids stimulates the liver and pancreas, providing a natural laxative action.

Many dogs enjoy fruits as a snack or as a regular part of their diet. Try out some of the following fruits with your dog to see which he or she prefers. Blueberries, apples and papaya are Lily's favourites!

Apple

Apples stimulate the appetite and remedy indigestion. This ability is due in part to the presence of malic and tartaric acids in apples, which inhibit the growth of disease-producing bacteria in the digestive tracts. Apples contain pectin, which helps detoxify the body from the effects of everyday pollution. Apples and their juice are also cleansing and beneficial for the liver and gall bladder.

Banana

A nutritional powerhouse, bananas are a rich source of potassium, which benefits the nervous and muscular systems (no wonder tennis players eat them!). They have a soothing effect on the gastrointestinal system, so are especially useful for stomach ulcers, and are said to help promote sleep. Always wait until they are fully ripe before using.

Blueberry

Known for their very high antioxidant content and anti-aging properties, blueberries contain anthocyanins, which have anti-inflammatory and anti-cancer properties. Blueberries are also good for the brain – new research in people shows that blueberries may help to slow signs of cognitive decline (Alzheimers).

Melon

An excellent cleanser and rehydrator, melon is a good fruit to use in the summer months. (Remove the seeds before using.)

Water

We are now all conditioned to drink plenty of water every day and the same is true for dogs. Water is, of course, really important to keep your dog well hydrated and to make sure their kidneys are being regularly flushed out. Change the water in your dog's bowl at least once a day. Lily is especially fussy about this!

Orange

Oranges aid digestion and help alleviate trapped wind. They are an excellent source of vitamin C (when used fresh), which benefits the immune system.

Papaya

An extremely nutrient-dense fruit, especially rich in vitamins A and C as well as potassium, calcium, phosphorus and iron, papaya cleanses the digestive tract, eliminating indigestion, reducing gas, soothing inflammation and cleansing and detoxifying the whole body. Papaya is good for dogs recovering from any digestive upset.

Raspberry

Of benefit to the liver and kidneys, enriching and cleansing the blood of toxins, raspberries help control urinary function and are said to help relieve excessive and frequent urination, especially at night. They are also reputed to help improve vision.

Strawberry

Rich in silica and vitamin C, strawberries are useful for connective tissue and blood vessel repair. They also improve appetite and are said to help relieve urinary difficulties.

How to read a dog food label

It's handy to know what to look out for when you are looking for a ready-made food for your dog. Price is generally a good indicator: if a food is cheap, it's because it's made with cheap ingredients. Buying the best you can afford for your dog will be worth it in the long term – their health and happiness depend on it!

Dry food

Dry foods were invented as a way of getting rid of waste material that food factories W not get properly absorbed and just go through the body.

Here's an indication of what those ingredients on the label actually mean, so that you can navigate your way through the pet food aisle and choose exactly the kind of food you want your dog to eat.

> " **Buying the best you can afford for your dog will be worth it in the long term.** "

Chicken meal/powdered chicken/ dry chicken/cooked chicken

These are all descriptions for an ingredient that is used in every dry food on the market today. Chicken meal is made by boiling chicken by-products such as carcase, skin and feathers, siphoning off the fat to make tallow, and what is left is dried at a very high temperature and then ground to a fine powder to resemble dark sand. It produces a high level of protein but dogs have trouble digesting it. This together with poor ingredients is what makes your dog windy. Meat meal is preserved with very heavy-duty artificial preservatives. When you are looking for a really good dry food, look for one that has a high level of fresh meat, rather than meat meal.

• No Substitute For Brushing! •

Some vets will tell you that dogs must eat only dry food so that they get their teeth cleaned. But this alone won't ensure clean teeth. If you speak to the vet nurse, he or she will tell you that the only thing that really keeps your dog's teeth clean is regular brushing!

Ash

The percentage of ash provides a helpful indicator of the quality of the dry food you are buying. The lower the ash content, the better: look for a dry food that has a low ash content – ideally between three and four per cent. Any dry food that contains more than five per cent ash will have a lot of chicken meal in it (see page 25). More than eight per cent ash is a worrying amount.

Tomato pomace

This is simply tomato skins, which, as any nutritionist will tell you, are not digestible.

> **Most dry foods have a long list of chemical additives added to preserve them.**

Oils and fats

Dogs love fat! It's cheap and it's tasty – and it's the only thing that tastes good to them in a kibble. Fat is sprayed onto the outside of the kibble so that they will eat the whole thing. Some dogs have worked this out and just lick the outside. Around eight to ten per cent fat content is healthy; dry food containing more than 12 per cent should be avoided.

Additives

Most dry foods have a long list of chemical additives added to preserve them. The worst offenders are the semi-moist dry foods that have to have lots of preservatives to stop the moist pieces going mouldy. The statement 'No added preservatives, colours or flavourings' on a label may, in fact, be meaningless, as only the ingredients added during manufacturing legally have to be declared, not the preservatives that have been added to these ingredients before they arrive in the factory!

Top Tip

Never feed your dog cooked bones as they are likely to splinter and get stuck in his or her throat. Feed big raw bones and submerge them in boiling water for a minute to kill off the surface bacteria. Never leave your dog unsupervised with a bone.

Wet foods

Choose one with lots of whole ingredients – pieces of food that you would recognize – chunks of real meat and real vegetables. Ideally, you want a food that resembles something you would make at home, but that is also a complete food, i.e. with the precise balance of ingredients and nutrients.

Most wet foods are made either as a 'chunk and jelly' or as a 'chunk and gravy'. When I first fed Lily wet food, I thought that the chunks in wet food were in fact pieces of meat; however they had no meat in them at all! What are made to look like chunks of meat are in fact waste products and flour that have been formed into chunks.

The 'gravy' or 'jelly' is usually a highly flavoured water-based fluid that usually contains a wide variety of additives and sweeteners to entice your dog to eat it.

Energy requirements for an active dog

It's handy to have a rough idea of how many calories your dog needs every day, although this varies between dogs depending on their metabolism and energy requirements. You need to take age into account, too: old dogs generally need up to 20 per cent less food than younger ones.

The best judge of how much to feed your pet is you. Weighing your dog every month or so will enable you to keep an eye on any weight gain or loss and decrease or increase the amount you're feeding accordingly. It's also a good idea to get an objective view: we tend to look at our pets adoringly and may not notice if they are a little overweight! Ask your vet's opinion on the weight your dog should be maintaining.

The table below gives an estimate of how many calories your dog should need on a daily basis.

Weight (kg/lb)	Active Kcal	Resting Kcal
5 (11)	374	234
6 (13)	429	268
7 (15½)	481	301
8 (17½)	532	332
9 (19¾)	581	363
10 (22)	629	393
11 (24¼)	676	422
12 (26½)	722	451
13 (28¾)	766	479
14 (30¾)	810	506
15 (33)	853	533
16 (35¼)	896	560
17 (37½)	937	586
18 (39¾)	978	611
19 (42)	1012	637
20 (44)	1059	662
21 (46¼)	1098	686
22 (48½)	1137	711
23 (50¾)	1176	735
24 (53)	1214	759
25 (55)	1252	782

what not to feed your dog

Here is a list of things your dog should not eat. If for some reason, he or she does get hold of any of these items and eat them, you should call your vet for advice on what to do.

Alcohol

Alcohol has a very toxic effect on dogs and can make them very sick.

Artificial sweeteners

They are easy to forget about, but artificial sweeteners can have an immediately fatal effect on dogs. A lady once phoned us in tears: her dog had died because she had given him the rest of her cereal to finish and she had sweetened it with artificial sweetener.

Avocado

Avocados are very high in fat and can cause digestive problems in dogs. They contain a chemical that can be toxic to some dogs and harm their liver, heart and lungs.

Chocolate

Even 50 g (2 oz) of chocolate can be fatal for a dog because it contains an ingredient called theobromide, which is incredibly toxic to dogs. It will be a slow and painful death, too, so if you suspect your dog has had chocolate, you do need to take him or her immediately to the vet to be given an antidote.

Coffee

Caffeine is harmful for dogs and can cause seizures. (Chocolate-covered espresso beans are particularly toxic for dogs.)

Grapes and raisins

A particular mould that can grow on grapes is very harmful to dogs and can even prove fatal.

Onions

Another food to avoid, onions can cause anaemia in dogs.

Top Tip

Make sure that you remove stones and pips from fruit such as apples, plums, peaches and cherries before feeding these fruits to your dog.

Puppy power!

> Puppies need to eat several times a day as they have small stomachs.

It was wonderful to watch Lily with her puppies, instinctively knowing exactly what to do – no training needed at all! Her children are now four years old and the picture of health!

Many owners give their new puppy food that has been given to them by the breeder. Bear in mind, however, that many breeders are sponsored by pet food companies. Do your research before you start automatically feeding your new puppy what the breeder has recommended; there may be much better alternatives for the new member of your family.

Puppies do need to eat several times a day as they have small stomachs and need lots of nutrition. Ideally pups that are four months old should be fed four times a day, then three times a day until they are six months old.

After that, you can begin to feed them twice a day like an adult dog. Puppies should grow at the right rate for their breed – not too quickly and not too slowly.

The recipes in this book can be used for puppies, but only alongside a specific diet that has been formulated especially for puppies. Pups need a balanced diet that includes appropriate amounts of calcium to ensure good bone formation and this is best provided by a specialist diet until they are six months old.

The treats in this book are perfect for puppies as they don't contain the usual array of hidden preservatives and additives. They are naturally delicious and nutritious and will be invaluable in training your puppy in good habits and getting rid of the bad ones!

Poop!

Your dog's poop is a very important issue – it's your daily indicator of how your dog is doing and whether he or she is digesting food well. In addition, of course, you need your dog's poop to be easy to pick up – that means nice and firm.

Many dog owners are nervous about straying away from a 'complete dry food' because they are worried that the poop will be too soft. Well, the good news is that a good-quality wet food or home-made food is easy to pick up because it's made with whole ingredients that have been properly digested, so what comes out is the waste and fibre rather than what seems like the same weight of ingredients that went into the bowl in the first place.

When you feed a low-quality food, your dog produces rather a lot of poop! Many ingredients in commercial pet foods cannot be broken down and digested by your dog's digestive system, so there's a big pile of poop to clean up. One of the first things people notice when feeding a home diet is that the volume of poop goes down and even that it smells better.

Some things to look out for: if the stools are soft but hold their shape then everything should be in good order. If they are too loose to pick up then your dog may have eaten something that doesn't agree with him or her. Very dark or black stools could mean that he or she has had a bit too much meat; get back to a balanced diet of meat, veg and some carbohydrates.

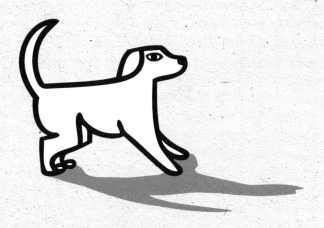

Banana Smoothie

Dogs love the taste and texture of bananas – just make sure the banana is ripe. I love using blueberries wherever I can (we generally use fresh ones in our recipes at Lily's Kitchen), partly because they are one of Lily's favourite things to eat, but also because they are jam-packed with vitamin C and lots of antioxidants. This is a yummy recipe to make for a Sunday breakfast.

················ ❀ ················

½ ripe banana
50 g (2 oz) blueberries
100 g (4 oz) natural probiotic yoghurt
1 tbsp ground flaxseed

················ ❀ ················

Put all the ingredients in a bowl and mash together.
Serve immediately.

················ ❀ ················

Kcals/100 g (4 oz): 115
Protein: 5%
Fat: 5%

Morning Porridge

Oats are a wonderful ingredient as they are very digestible and also high in protein. This makes a satisfying and healthy start to the day.

· · · · · · · · · · · · · · ❀ · · · · · · · · · · · · · ·

100 g (4 oz) oats
1 apple
small handful blueberries
1 tbsp ground flaxseed
1 tsp dried (or 1 tbsp finely chopped fresh) herbs (see pages 122–3)

· · · · · · · · · · · · · · ❀ · · · · · · · · · · · · · ·

Put the oats in a saucepan and pour over 600 ml (1 pint) water. Cover and simmer cook for 5 minutes. Leave to cool completely (this can take about an hour, so you might want to cook the oats the night before, cover and leave overnight to cool).

Grate the apple and stir into the cooked oats, along with the blueberries, flaxseed and herbs.

· · · · · · · · · · · · · · ❀ · · · · · · · · · · · · · ·

Kcals/100 g (4 oz): 360
Protein: 10%
Fat: 8%

Variations

Stir 250 g (9 oz) cottage cheese into the cooked oats along with the fruit and herbs
Add 2 beaten eggs to the oats before cooking
Add 100 g (4 oz) cooked, diced chicken or turkey
Mix 1 x 200g tin of salmon in oil into the finished porridge

Apple and Blueberry Muffins

These are a yummy – and very healthy – treat to share with your dog, although they won't be as sweet as you're probably used to. I've added cottage cheese to this recipe to give a little boost of protein.

Break up the muffins to give them to your dog rather than feeding them whole. They'll last longer that way too! (They should keep fresh for up to 3 days if stored in an airtight container.)

············· ✿ ·············

Makes 20 mini muffins or 10 large ones

150 g (5 oz) brown rice flour (or wholewheat flour)
2 eggs
100 ml (4 fl oz) milk
2 tbsp olive oil
50 g (2 oz) cottage cheese
2 small, sweet eating apples, peeled, cored and grated
50 g (2 oz) blueberries
1 tbsp ground flaxseed
1 tsp dried (or 1 tbsp finely chopped fresh) herbs (see pages 122–3)
1 tsp honey (optional)

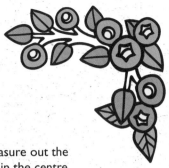

· · · · · · · · · · · · · · ⊗ · · · · · · · · · · · · · ·

Preheat the oven to 180°C (350°F/gas mark 4). Measure out the brown rice flour into a clean bowl and form a well in the centre. Break the eggs into another bowl, pour in the milk and olive oil and beat lightly together. Pour this mixture into the well in the brown rice flour and stir in. You should have a nice loose mixture.

Stir in the cottage cheese, grated apple, blueberries, ground flaxseed and herbs. If you want to sweeten the recipe, add a teaspoon of honey. Mix together thoroughly with a spoon.

Lightly grease a muffin or bun tin and spoon a tablespoon of the mixture into each of the holes. Place the tin into the preheated oven and bake for 20 minutes.

· · · · · · · · · · · · · · ⊗ · · · · · · · · · · · · · ·

Kcals/100 g (4 oz): 365
Protein: 14%
Fat: 9%

Fruit Salad

It is good to serve your dog fruit as it provides so many health benefits, including lots of vitamin C and antioxidants. It's also a good source of soluble fibre – so good for digestion too.

················· ❁ ·················

1 ripe banana
1 apple
100 g (4 oz) blueberries

················· ❁ ·················

Peel and chop the banana, core and chop the apple and mix both together with the blueberries in your dog's bowl.

················· ❁ ·················

Kcals/100 g (4 oz): 70
Protein: 1%
Fat: 0%

· Top Tip ·

Serve this as a snack rather than as a dessert (i.e. as an additional dish) as fruit could ferment in your dog's stomach and cause wind or indigestion if eaten straight after a meaty meal.

Savoury Porridge

Lentils and oats make an excellent combination as they are both high in protein and low GI, which means they will help your dog feel satisfied for longer, thus – hopefully – eliminating any begging behaviour!

Lentils are extremely digestible and so are oats. If this is the very first time you are feeding your dog lentils, then you may get some wind, but once he or she gets used to digesting whole food, rather than the usual list of animal derivatives and chicken meal present in most pet foods, this should cease to be a problem.

· · · · · · · · · · · · · 🐾 · · · · · · · · · · · · ·

200 g (7 oz) of lentils
75 g (3 oz) porridge oats
100 g (4 oz) cottage cheese
1 tsp finely chopped fresh parsley
250 g (9 oz) cooked meat (turkey, chicken, beef or fish), chopped

· · · · · · · · · · · · · 🐾 · · · · · · · · · · · · ·

Put the lentils in a pan and cover with about 900 ml water (1 ½ pints). Bring to the boil and simmer gently for about 25 minutes or until cooked.

Once they have cooked just add in the oats, stir and leave to cool.

Stir in the cottage cheese (you should have a thick purée), the parsley and then the chopped cooked meat.

You can either form the mixture into patties and place on a plate, or store it in the bowl to use as and when you need it.

· · · · · · · · · · · · · 🐾 · · · · · · · · · · · · ·

Kcals/100 g (4 oz): 440
Protein: 20%
Fat: 11%

Frittata

Eggs are a really good source of complete protein for dogs. Eggs are better cooked, as raw eggs contain an enzyme that stops the absorption of Vitamin B and can also carry the risk of salmonella.

This is a good recipe to make on those days when you open your dog's cupboard and it's bare – and you can whip it up in no time. If you are very pressed for time, you could just serve the eggs on their own as a scramble.

· · · · · · · · · · · · · ❀ · · · · · · · · · · · · ·

200 g (7 oz) potatoes, peeled and roughly chopped
50 g (2 oz) peas (frozen or fresh)
1 tbsp vegetable oil
2 eggs, beaten

· · · · · · · · · · · · · ❀ · · · · · · · · · · · · ·

Put the chopped potatoes in a pan of boiling water and simmer until cooked. Drain.

Cook the peas in a separate pan of boiling water for a few minutes until done.

Heat the vegetable oil in a frying pan, then pour in the beaten eggs. Place the peas and potatoes on top and cook for 2 minutes. Fold the frittata in half and continue to cook for a further 2–3 minutes until the eggs are done.

Remove the pan from the heat and leave to cool for several minutes until the frittata reaches room temperature. Chop up and serve.

· · · · · · · · · · · · · ❀ · · · · · · · · · · · · ·

Kcals/100 g (4 oz): 360
Protein: 21%
Fat: 12%

Healthy Mealtimes

• We all think that dogs have stomachs of steel, but they can also get sick from food-borne illnesses that affect people. Here are some things you can do to ensure your dog stays as healthy as possible:

• Always wash your hands before your prepare your dog's food

• Cook meat thoroughly

• Store cooked meat and raw meat separately from each other and from other foods

• Once you have thawed out a food, do not refreeze

• If you put food out for your dog and he or she does not eat it, then do not leave out it for longer than two hours; discard it

• Always keep your dog's food bowl and water bowl clean; wash them after every meal.

Buckwheat Pancakes

Buckwheat is a lovely flour – it has a sweet taste and is also very nutritious. These are easy pancakes to make and you can fill them with all sorts of things to create a nutritious meal. This is also a rather good recipe to share!

200 g (7 oz) buckwheat flour
500 ml (17 fl oz) milk
2 eggs, beaten
1 tsp vegetable oil

For the filling:
100 g (4 oz) cottage cheese
100 g (4 oz) spinach leaves, shredded

Measure out the flour into a bowl, make a well in the centre and pour in the milk and beaten eggs. Whisk together, then place the bowl into the fridge for 20 minutes.

Heat the vegetable oil in a frying pan, then pour enough batter into the pan to coat the bottom. Cook for about 30 seconds, then flip the pancake over and cook for a further minute or so.

Put the cottage cheese in the centre of the pancake and add the spinach leaves. Roll up the pancake while it's in the pan so the filling heats up. Cut into pieces to serve.

Without/including filling:
Kcals/100 g (4 oz): 328/347
Protein: 13%/16%
Fat: 32%/32%

Variations

Replace the spinach leaves and cottage
cheese with one of the following:
50 g (2 oz) grated Cheddar cheese
50 g (2 oz) cream cheese
50 g (2 oz) lean chopped ham

Daily Dinners

Homemade Kibble

This is a great dish as all of the ingredients, except the turkey, are made in one pot. You could, of course, just serve this as a stew, but I love the idea of being able to make your own kibble. It does take about an hour to make, but it's very easy, and also very empowering to make a food that always seems to be a bit of an industry secret.

Turkey is great as it's very low in fat as well as being very digestible, which makes it useful for dogs that are allergic to the usual protein sources – lamb, beef and chicken. Turkey is also handy as it's readily available minced (unlike chicken!).

This is also a good hypo-allergenic recipe as it is free from wheat. You'll notice I haven't included peas, which seem always to be part of a dog's menu these days. Peas can be quite hard to digest for some dogs and therefore can make your dog rather windy.

· · · · · · · · · · · · · · ❁ · · · · · · · · · · · · · ·

200 g (7 oz) brown rice
100 g (4 oz) lentils
200 g (7 oz) carrots, peeled and chopped
200 g (7 oz) sweet potato, scrubbed and chopped
1 apple, peeled, cored and chopped, or 100 g (4 oz) apple purée
100 g (4 oz) whole oats
1 tbsp finely chopped fresh parsley
2 small sprigs of fresh rosemary, finely chopped
500 g (1 lb 2 oz) minced turkey
50 ml (2 fl oz) olive, sunflower or rapeseed oil

· · · · · · · · · · · · · · ❁ · · · · · · · · · · · · · ·

Put the rice and lentils into a saucepan and cover with 1.2 litres (2 pints) of water. Bring to the boil, then reduce the heat and simmer for 20 minutes. Drain, return to the saucepan and set aside. Preheat the oven to 180°C (350°F/gas 4).

Add the chopped carrots, sweet potato and apple to the saucepan of rice and lentils. Stir in the oats and chopped herbs and cook on a gentle simmer for a further 20 minutes.

Meanwhile, brown the turkey mince in a separate frying pan. You will need to keep stirring it while it is cooking to prevent it sticking to the pan as it is very low in fat. It will take about 10 minutes to cook through.

Put half the cooked vegetable and grain mixture into a food processor with half the cooked turkey, add half the oil and blitz so that it resembles a thick purée.

Spread this mixture onto a baking sheet so that it is about 5 mm (¼ in) thick. The mixture will spread slightly so leave a bit of room for this.

Repeat as above with the remaining ingredients.

Place both baking sheets into the preheated oven for 35–45 minutes, flipping it over half way through the cooking time to make sure it's cooked on both sides. (It's important to flip it over so that it dries through.) You should have what looks like two very large cookies. Make sure that the kibble is completely cooked through, as any moist bits will go mouldy after a couple of days.

Reduce the oven temperature to 160°C (325°F/gas 3), remove the baking sheets from the oven and cut the 'kibble cookies' into small pieces. Replace the baking sheets with the broken pieces on them into the oven for 1 hour until they are completely dry (but not burnt).

Remove the kibble from the oven and leave to cool completely. It should resemble pieces of broken pitta bread. It will keep in the fridge for 10 days.

· · · · · · · · · · · · ✿ · · · · · · · · · · · · ·

Kcals/100 g (4 oz): 365
Protein: 20%
Fat: 9%

Variations

Use chickpeas as a substitute for the lentils and/or quinoa instead of rice.
Substitute the vegetables used here for any others listed on pages 20–1.
Replace the herbs with others from the list on pages 122–3.

Salmon and Oat Balls

This easy no-cook recipe is a great way to give your dog some fish containing the important omega-3 essential fatty acids. (For an extra omega boost, add in a tablespoon of ground flaxseed.) The soft bones in the salmon are also a good source of calcium. The rosehips here provide a lovely, natural form of vitamin C, while kelp is a rich source of nutrients. This is a good recipe for a sick dog, too.

· · · · · · · · · · · · ·✺· · · · · · · · · · · · ·

100 g (4 oz) porridge oats
1 x 200 g tin of salmon in oil
1 carrot, peeled and grated
1 apple, peeled, cored and grated
¼ tsp ground rosehip
¼ tsp kelp
2 tbsp oil

· · · · · · · · · · · · ·✺· · · · · · · · · · · · ·

Soak the oats in 100 ml (4 fl oz) of water for 15 minutes (this makes them more digestible for your dog).

Empty the tin of salmon, including the oil, into a bowl and mash up with a fork. (You don't need to remove the pieces of bone – they will dissolve and are a great source of calcium for your dog.)

Add the soaked oats, grated carrot and apple, rosehip, kelp and oil and stir together well.

Roll the mixture into small balls in your hands. They will keep for 5 days in the fridge or up to 2 months in the freezer.

· · · · · · · · · · · · ·✺· · · · · · · · · · · · ·

Kcals/100 g (4 oz): 200
Protein: 11%
Fat: 9%

Sardine Bake

This is a great recipe for dogs that need some time off from meat! Sardines are a fantastic source of omega-3 essential fatty acids and are rich in protein, helping to maintain strong and healthy bones. They are also the best source of vitamin B12 of all fish.

· · · · · · · · · · · · · · 🐾 · · · · · · · · · · · · · ·

oil for greasing
1 x 120 g tin sardines in oil
400 g (14 oz) potatoes, peeled and thinly sliced
50 g (2 oz) peas (fresh or frozen)

· · · · · · · · · · · · · · 🐾 · · · · · · · · · · · · · ·

Preheat the oven to 180°C (350°F/gas mark 4). Lightly grease an ovenproof dish.

Put the sardines and their oil into a small bowl and mash. Lay half the potato slices in the bottom of the dish, cover with the mashed sardines and peas, then finish with the remainder of the potato slices.

Cover the dish with foil and bake in the oven for 30 minutes until cooked through.

Allow to cool to room temperature before serving. It will keep, covered, in the fridge for up to 4 days.

· · · · · · · · · · · · · · 🐾 · · · · · · · · · · · · · ·

Kcals/100 g (4 oz): 350
Protein: 23%
Fat: 10%

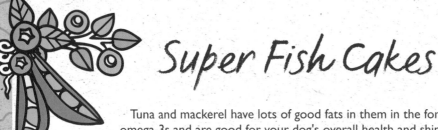

Super Fish Cakes

Tuna and mackerel have lots of good fats in them in the form of omega-3s and are good for your dog's overall health and shiny coat. Dogs also love the taste of fish and it's great to give them a spectrum of proteins, rather than just relying on chicken and lamb.

· · · · · · · · · · · · · · ❀ · · · · · · · · · · · · · ·

500 g (1 lb 2 oz) potatoes, peeled and diced
50 g (2 oz) broccoli, chopped
1 tin tuna in oil
1 tin mackerel in oil
1 tbsp finely chopped fresh parsley

· · · · · · · · · · · · · · ❀ · · · · · · · · · · · · · ·

Put the potatoes in a saucepan and cover with water. Bring to the boil, then reduce the heat and simmer for 20 minutes until cooked. Place the broccoli in with the potatoes for the last 5 minutes of cooking. Drain the vegetables and mash them roughly.

Add the tinned tuna and mackerel, along with their oils, and the parsley and stir together well.

Leave to cool completely then form into balls. Cover with cling film and place in the fridge. These will keep fresh in the fridge for up to 5 days.

· · · · · · · · · · · · · · ❀ · · · · · · · · · · · · · ·

Kcals/100 g (4 oz): 380
Protein: 30%
Fat: 13%

Variations

Replace the potato with butternut squash,
peeled, seeded and chopped.
Replace the broccoli with spinach.

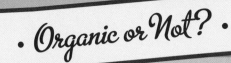

Organic or Not?

Ideally you would always use organic ingredients when making food for your dog. Unfortunately, the cost of some organic ingredients can sometimes be rather high, so as long as you are happy with the food choices you are making then the ingredients you choose will be fine – and still much better than something cooked up by a mass-produced pet food company (apart from ours, of course!)

Here are some key facts about organic ingredients:

• Animals that are reared organically have a better quality of life as they are free to roam outdoors, in their natural habitat

• No pesticides are used on foods or grass that these animals eat

• Hormones and antibiotics are not allowed except in exceptional circumstances

• Organic production usually has a much lower yield as animals and pastures have not been pumped up with steroids, fertilizers and other artificial additives

• Organic farming is better for the environment in general – fewer pesticides and artificial fertilizers means more wildlife and a better overall eco-system

• Organic certification is a guarantee that no genetically modified ingredients have been used and no artificial ingredients have been used that have not been previously approved by the certifier.

Wonderful One-pot

This is a good, satisfying recipe that contains a wide range of yummy nutrients. There's a rainbow of fruits and vegetables here, too, together with the ideal combination of lentils, rice and oats. Spoon out however much you need for your dog's meal.

Broccoli is a super vegetable for dogs that is full of nutrition as well as helpful against cancer, but Lily tends to leave behind a neat pile of it in her bowl unless I chop it up very finely!

· · · · · · · · · · · · · ✿ · · · · · · · · · · · · · ·

100 g (4 oz) brown rice
100 g (4 oz) lentils
50 g (2 oz) oats
2 tbsp olive oil
300 g (11 oz) boned chicken thighs, diced
200 g (7 oz) carrots, peeled and finely diced
100 g (4 oz) broccoli, finely chopped
2 x 200g tins of salmon
200 g (7 oz) apples, peeled, cored and grated
50 g (2 oz) blueberries
1 tbsp ground flaxseed

· · · · · · · · · · · · · ✿ · · · · · · · · · · · · · ·

Rinse the brown rice and lentils under cold running water. It is best to soak them overnight and then rinse, as they're more digestible that way, but don't worry if you don't have time.

Put the rice and lentils into a saucepan and add 1 litre (1¾ pints) of cold water. Bring to the boil, then reduce the heat, cover and simmer gently for 30 minutes until they are cooked. Stir in the oats and leave for 5 minutes.

Heat 1 teaspoon of the olive oil in a frying pan, add the diced chicken and cook for 10 minutes.

Meanwhile, put the carrots into a pan of simmering water and cook for 5 minutes, then add the broccoli and cook for a further 5 minutes. Drain.

Open the cans of salmon and fork gently. Don't worry about the bones as they will be soft and a very good source of calcium for your dog.

Put the grated apples and blueberries into a large bowl and stir in all the other ingredients. This will keep in the fridge for up to 4 days.

.... ✿ ....

Kcals/100 g (4 oz): 400
Protein: 25%
Fat: 18%

Top Tip

Never feed your dog raw salmon as this can contain parasites that are particularly harmful to dogs.

Chicken and Rice Balls

If you have a dog that seems to get on best with bland food, then this is a good recipe to make. There's a good balance of vegetables, carbohydrate and protein. If your have dog is overweight or has an intolerance to fat, then discard the skin of the chicken after it has been cooked. This is a good recipe for a poorly dog, too.

· · · · · · · · · · · · · ❀ · · · · · · · · · · · · ·

4 or 5 chicken thighs
200 g (7 oz) carrots, chopped
200 g (7 oz) parsnips, chopped
100 g (4 oz) rice
1 tsp finely chopped fresh parsley or rosemary
50 g (2 oz) porridge oats

· · · · · · · · · · · · · ❀ · · · · · · · · · · · · ·

Put the chicken thighs in a saucepan and cover with water. Bring to the boil then reduce the heat and simmer for 20 minutes.

Put the chopped carrots and parsnips into a clean pan, cover with water and bring to the boil. Reduce the heat and simmer until soft. Drain, then return the vegetables to the pan and mash together.

Put the rice in a saucepan with 300 ml (½ pint) of water, bring to the boil, then cover and simmer until cooked. (Follow packet instructions as cooking times vary depending on the type of rice.)

Once the chicken is cooked, drain and reserve the stock, remove the bones from the thighs and chop the meat and skin into small pieces.

Put the chicken pieces into a bowl with the cooked rice, mashed vegetables and dried herbs and mix together well.

Spread the porridge oats out on a large plate. Form the chicken, rice and vegetable mixture into small balls and roll them in the oats to coat.

The finished chicken and rice balls can be stored in the fridge for up to 5 days or you can freeze them for 2 months.

· · · · · · · · · · · · · ❁ · · · · · · · · · · · · ·

Kcals/100 g (4 oz): 400
Protein: 20%
Fat: 18%

Top Tip

Keep the stock as it will be full of goodness. Keep it in the fridge for up to a week to use for another recipe, such as the porridge ones (see pages 35 and 105).

Rice with Meat

This is a good easy recipe and one that is a favourite in our household. As with most of the recipes in this book, it's wheat gluten free.

· · · · · · · · · · · · · · ✤ · · · · · · · · · · · · · ·

A few drops of sunflower oil
450 g (1 lb) minced beef
200 g (7 oz) rice
85 g (3 oz) spinach
2 grated carrots
1 tsp finely chopped fresh parsley
50 ml (2 fl oz) natural yoghurt (optional)

· · · · · · · · · · · · · · ✤ · · · · · · · · · · · · · ·

Heat a few drops of sunflower oil in a frying pan then brown the mince, breaking it up with a wooden spoon.

Add the rice, spinach, grated carrots, parsley and 600 ml (1 pint) water. Stir, then cover and cook on a gentle simmer until the water has been absorbed by the rice – this usually takes about 20 minutes.

Remove the lid and leave to cool. Store in the fridge for up to 5 days.

Before serving, you can stir in a tablespoon of natural yoghurt for some extra probiotic goodness, if you wish.

· · · · · · · · · · · · · · ✤ · · · · · · · · · · · · · ·

Kcals/100 g (4 oz): 400
Protein: 22%
Fat: 17%

Variations

Replace the beef mince with minced turkey, lamb, chicken or pork.

Sunshine Stew

This is a lovely, colourful and very satisfying stew. I've used lamb, but you could also use turkey, beef or chicken mince. I've added some liver, too, to provide some extra nutrition and taste.

................⊗................

200 g (7 oz) lentils (green or red)
100 g (4 oz) pearl barley
1 butternut squash, peeled, seeded and diced
100 g (4 oz) green beans, trimmed and chopped
400 g (14 oz) lamb mince
200 g (7 oz) chicken livers, chopped
1 tbsp salmon oil or flaxseed oil
1 tsp dried (or 1 tbsp finely chopped fresh) herbs (see pages 122–3)

................⊗................

Rinse the lentils and pearl barley and put in a saucepan with 1 litre (1¾ pints) of water. Bring to the boil, reduce the heat and simmer for 30 minutes. Drain.

Meanwhile, put the butternut squash and beans into another pan and cover with water. Bring to the boil, reduce the heat and simmer gently for 20 minutes.

Put the lamb mince and chopped chicken livers into a frying pan and fry gently for 15 minutes until cooked through.

Combine all the cooked ingredients and mix together. Stir in the salmon or flaxseed oil. Add the herbs.

You can either serve this as a stew, or process it lightly in a food processor if your dog tends to leave the veggies and just go for the meat! If you process it, you can roll the mixture into balls and keep in the fridge for 5 days or freezer for 2 months and just pull out the amount you need for a meal.

................⊗................

Kcals/100 g (4 oz): 330
Protein: 32%
Fat: 7%

Lamb, Lentil and Vegetable Stew

This is a lovely wholesome stew that is satisfying to make for your dog on a rainy afternoon. It contains a super variety of fruits and vegetables and is low in fat.

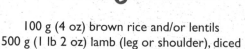

100 g (4 oz) brown rice and/or lentils
500 g (1 lb 2 oz) lamb (leg or shoulder), diced
50 g (2 oz) chicken livers, chopped
½ butternut squash, peeled and diced
50 g (2 oz) peas
1 head of broccoli, broken into segments and/or chopped
2 sweet eating apples, peeled, cored and diced
50 g (2 oz) fresh spinach, shredded
50 g (2 oz) blueberries
1 tbsp ground flaxseed
1 tsp dried (or 1 tbsp finely chopped fresh) herbs (see pages 122–3)

Rinse the brown rice and/or lentils in cold water then put in a large saucepan with 700 ml (1¼ pints) of cold water. Bring to the boil, then reduce the heat and simmer for 10 minutes.

Add the chopped lamb and chicken livers to the saucepan (make sure there is enough water) and cook for 10 minutes.

Add the squash to the saucepan and cook for 15 minutes. Add the peas, broccoli, apples and spinach leaves and cook for a further 15 minutes.

Finally, add the blueberries and cook for a further 5 minutes.

Remove the pan from the heat and stir in the ground flaxseed and herbs. Leave to cool to room temperature before serving. Any remaining stew can be refrigerated for up to 3 days.

Kcals/100 g (4 oz): 500
Protein: 26%
Fat: 11%

Top Tip

If you want to include some extra fat because your dog needs building up then add a tablespoon of flaxseed oil and a tablespoon of salmon oil to each meal.

Meat Loaf

This is a very satisfying recipe to make as it looks and smells delicious. It's also rather handy as it will keep for several days in the fridge, so you can just slice it up and use it as you need it.

· · · · · · · · · · · · ✿ · · · · · · · · · · · ·

200 g (7 oz) chicken livers
450 g (1 lb) minced beef
400 g (14 oz) potatoes, peeled and grated
150 g (5 oz) carrots, peeled and grated
2 eggs
50 g (2 oz) oats
1 tbsp finely chopped fresh parsley and/or rosemary

· · · · · · · · · · · · ✿ · · · · · · · · · · · ·

Preheat the oven to 180°C (350°F/gas mark 4). Lightly cook the livers in simmering water for 3 minutes then drain and chop finely.

Put the mince in the bowl and stir in the grated potato and carrot and the chopped liver.

In a separate bowl, lightly beat the eggs, then add them to the mixture, along with the oats and herbs. Mix together with a spoon or clean hands.

Scoop the mixture into a well-greased loaf tin and lightly flatten the top. Bake in the preheated oven for 1–1½ hours.

Remove the meat loaf from the oven and leave to stand for 20 minutes or so to make it easier to slice.

It will keep in the fridge for a week or it can be frozen for up to 2 months.

Kcals/100 g (4 oz): 430
Protein: 31%
Fat: 20%

· Top Tip ·

You can also make this in greased muffin tins for individual portions. Reduce the cooking time to 50 minutes.

Traditional Gravy

This is a traditional gravy, but with no salt added and very low in fat. I've included a garlic clove; garlic in moderation is great for dogs as it's one of nature's pharmacy specials, full of beneficial properties. Because you sieve it out with the bones, your dog won't be digesting it, just benefiting from its healing properties. Kelp has abundant minerals and trace elements, as do many seaweeds.

· · · · · · · · · · · · · ❀ · · · · · · · · · · · · ·

500 g (1 lb 2 oz) of bones from your butcher
1 clove garlic, peeled
2 carrots, peeled and chopped
2 potatoes, peeled and chopped
½ tsp kelp

· · · · · · · · · · · · · ❀ · · · · · · · · · · · · ·

Put the bones in a large saucepan together with the peeled clove of garlic and add 2 litres (3½ pints) of water. Cover the pan, bring to the boil, then reduce the heat and simmer gently for an hour.

Put the carrots and potatoes into another pan and cover with water. Bring to the boil, then reduce the heat and simmer until soft. Drain, then mash or purée them.

Take the bones off the heat and then pour the mixture into a sieve over a clean saucepan. Discard everything that is left in the sieve. Add this stock to the mashed vegetables, then add the kelp and stir well to combine.

The gravy can be kept in the fridge for a week or you can freeze it in an ice-cube tray for up to 2 months and use as needed.

· · · · · · · · · · · · · ❀ · · · · · · · · · · · · ·

Kcals/100 g (4 oz): 60
Protein: 8%
Fat: 1%

Superfood Gravy

The gravies that we might enjoy are not good for your dog because they are far too salty. Here, instead, is a gravy that is perfect for dogs – meaty, rich, delicious and with some good antioxidants, so healthy as well. Organ meat in the form of liver gives it a vitamin E boost too.

It does take a bit of time to prepare, but you can then pour it into an ice-cube tray, freeze it and take out cubes to use as and when you need. The frozen gravy cubes will keep for up to two months. Warm to room temperature before feeding.

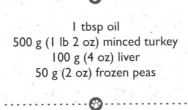

1 tbsp oil
500 g (1 lb 2 oz) minced turkey
100 g (4 oz) liver
50 g (2 oz) frozen peas

Heat the oil in a frying pan and brown the mince and livers.

Once the meats are browned, add the frozen peas, then pour in 700 ml (1¼ pints) water. Put a lid on the pan and leave to simmer for 30 minutes.

Remove the pan from the heat and leave to cool slightly, then place the mixture in a food processor or blender and blitz until smooth. It may still look a bit grainy once you have done this, but your dog won't mind!

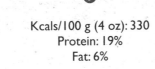

Kcals/100 g (4 oz): 330
Protein: 19%
Fat: 6%

· Special Meals ·

· for Special Days ·

Celebration Cupcakes

Our family famously invited my daughter's entire class over for a picnic on the local heath to celebrate Lily's first birthday (to the horror of the school's new headmistress, who was appalled to think she had joined the kind of school where even dogs' birthdays were celebrated!). I served these cupcakes to Lily and her friends, who devoured them all! They look very appetizing and are also very healthy.

· · · · · · · · · · · · · ❀ · · · · · · · · · · · · ·

Makes 6

150 g (5 oz) brown rice flour
2 eggs
100 ml (4 fl oz) milk
2 tbsp olive oil
50 g (2 oz) Cheddar cheese, grated
1 tbsp ground flaxseed
1 tbsp finely chopped fresh parsley
50 g (2 oz) cream cheese

Preheat the oven to 180°C (350°F/gas 4). Lightly grease a muffin tin.

Measure out the brown rice flour into a clean bowl and make a well in the centre.

Break the eggs into another bowl and pour in the milk and olive oil. Beat lightly together. Add to the brown rice flour and stir well. You should have a nice loose mixture. Add the grated Cheddar cheese, herbs and ground flaxseed and mix together with a spoon.

Spoon 1½ tablespoons of the mixture into each hole of the muffin or bun tin. Transfer to the preheated oven and bake for 15 minutes until the tops are a light golden colour.

Remove the cupcakes from the oven and place on a wire rack to cool. Once they are completely cool, spread a teaspoon of cream cheese on the top of each cupcake.

Kcals/100 g (4 oz): 445
Protein: 16%
Fat: 20%

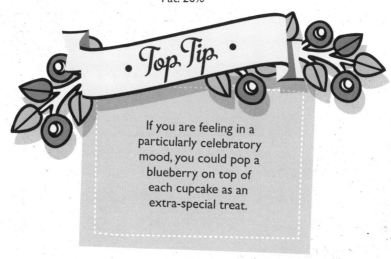

Top Tip

If you are feeling in a particularly celebratory mood, you could pop a blueberry on top of each cupcake as an extra-special treat.

Birthday Cake

We love celebrating Lily's birthday by making her something extra special. This is a really good recipe that is easy to slice up and share with any other doggy friends that are invited over for tea. You can also decorate it easily so that the cake looks appealing and appetizing ... though Lily, of course, doesn't really care what it looks like as long as it tastes delicious!

· · · · · · · · · · · · · · ❁ · · · · · · · · · · · · · ·

300 g (11 oz) minced lamb
200 g (7 oz) flour
50 g (2 oz) oats
50 g (2 oz) ground sunflower seeds
100 g (4 oz) cottage cheese
2 eggs, beaten

To decorate:
150 g (5 oz) low-fat cream cheese
100 g (4 oz) Cheddar cheese slices, cut into small squares
1 tbsp finely chopped parsley

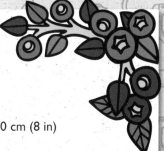

········•❀•·········

Preheat the oven to 180°C (350°F/gas 4). Lightly grease a 20 cm (8 in) round cake tin.

Stir the minced lamb, flour, oats, ground sunflower seeds, cottage cheese and eggs into a bowl and mix together well.

Spoon the mixture into the prepared cake tin and bake the cake in the oven for about 45 minutes, until it is cooked through. Remove the cake from the oven, leave to stand for a few minutes and then remove from the tin and place on a wire rack to cool completely.

'Ice' the top of the cooled cake with low-fat cream cheese. Use the Cheddar cheese squares to decorate the top of the cake, then sprinkle over the chopped parsley.

········•❀•·········

Kcals/100 g (4 oz): 520
Protein: 23%
Fat: 27%

Christmas Feast

Christmas is always a feast of food that is quite rich and heavy. You will want to share the Christmas cheer with your pet, but try to avoid feeding him tidbits that are high in fat, such as cheese, sausages and ham. Ideally, keep the treats to mealtimes so that your beautifully trained dog doesn't turn into a scavenging wide-eyed beggar of food! Here's a Christmas dinner he can happily and healthily share with you.

· · · · · · · · · · · · · ·❀· · · · · · · · · · · · · ·

250 g (8 oz) cooked turkey
1 cooked chipolata sausage
100 g (4 oz) mashed potato
100 g (4 oz) cooked Brussels sprouts

· · · · · · · · · · · · · ·❀· · · · · · · · · · · · · ·

Chop up the turkey and sausage into small pieces and put in a bowl. Add the mashed potato and Brussels sprouts and mash together.

· · · · · · · · · · · · · ·❀· · · · · · · · · · · · · ·

Kcals/100 g (4 oz): 460
Protein: 33%
Fat: 25%

· Top Tip ·

You can add a maximum of 2 tablespoons of gravy, but avoid giving this to your dog if it has any alcohol in.

Lamb Cupcakes

These are a delicious meaty treat and ideal for special occasions when you know you will be having a few dogs visiting. It's easier not to use paper cases so you don't have to pull them off before feeding.

· · · · · · · · · · · · · 🐾 · · · · · · · · · · · · ·

Makes 12

500 g (1 lb 2 oz) minced lamb
200 g (7 oz) brown rice flour
50 g (2 oz) porridge oats
1 egg, beaten

· · · · · · · · · · · · · 🐾 · · · · · · · · · · · · ·

Preheat the oven to 180°C (350°F/gas 4). Lightly grease a bun tin.

Put all the ingredients into a bowl and mix together well.

Spoon a heaped tablespoon of the mixture into each hole of the bun tin, then bake for 30 minutes until cooked through.

Leave to cool completely before feeding. They will keep for 5 days in the fridge.

· · · · · · · · · · · · · 🐾 · · · · · · · · · · · · ·

Kcals/100 g (4 oz): 620
Protein: 30%
Fat: 13%

Top Tip

If you are making these for a special event, why not try 'icing' them with cream cheese and using alfalfa seeds as sprinkles?

Mince Pies

Mince pies are a traditional festive favourite. Unfortunately, the ones we humans love are filled with raisins (and sometimes alcohol), which dogs must not eat. So here is a recipe that they will love, so that they, too, have their own mince pies to eat during the holiday period.

I add ginger to this recipe as it's a good spice for joints and helpful, too, as a blood cleanser.

These pies are rather fattening as there's a lot of pastry in each pie so even though it is the festive season, feed only one or two a day, and if your dog has had two, then reduce his or her regular amount of food accordingly.

············🐾············

Makes 8

400 g (14 oz) turkey mince
1 tbsp finely chopped fresh parsley
¼ tsp ground ginger (optional)

For the pastry:
200 g (7 oz) plain flour
100 ml (4 fl oz) oil
1 egg, beaten
50 g (2 oz) grated cheese

Preheat the oven to 180°C (350°F/gas 4). Lightly grease a bun tin.

Put the turkey mince into a bowl and stir in the chopped parsley and ground ginger (if using). Set aside.

To make the pastry, measure out the flour into a bowl and add the oil, beaten egg and grated cheese. Stir together with a spoon.

Put the dough onto a lightly floured surface and roll out. Cut out the dough into rounds using a cookie or pastry cutter and use half these rounds to line 8 holes of the bun tin.

Add a teaspoon of the turkey mixture into each pastry case. Brush the edges of the remaining pastry rounds with water then use them to top each of the pies, pressing them gently around the edges to seal. Pierce the top of each pie with a fork to allow steam to escape while cooking.

Place the tin into the oven and cook for 30 minutes. Once cooked, remove the pies from the oven and put onto a wire rack to cool.

You can store these mince pies in the fridge for up to a week.

·········· ❀ ··········

Kcals/100 g (4 oz): 620
Protein: 28%
Fat: 13%

· Top Tip ·

If your dog is gluten intolerant, replace the wheat flour with spelt flour. The spelt dough is easy to handle but can be a little crumbly when cooked.

Hallowe'en Hotpot

Hallowe'en occurs (in the northern hemisphere, at least) when winter
is just around the corner. Lily's coat begins to look rather bushy
at this time of the year – she resembles a small woolly lamb – and
there's also a lot more huddling up around the fireplace or in front of
the cooker. It seems only right to make her something warming that
will help keep out the cold.

· · · · · · · · · · · · · 🐾 · · · · · · · · · · · · ·

400 g (14 oz) pumpkin
50 g (2 oz) rice
300 g (11 oz) minced lamb
1 tsp dried (or 1 tbsp finely chopped fresh) herbs (see pages 122–3)

· · · · · · · · · · · · · 🐾 · · · · · · · · · · · · ·

Preheat the oven to 180°C (350°F/gas 4).

Peel the pumpkin and chop the flesh into small pieces. Place in a
roasting tin and bake in the oven for 20–25 minutes.

Meanwhile, put the rice into a saucepan, cover with about 250 ml (8 fl oz) of boiling water and simmer until cooked. (Follow the packet instructions as cooking time will vary depending on the type of rice.)

Gently fry the minced lamb in a frying pan for 15 minutes, then stir in the herbs. Add the cooked rice and pumpkin to the pan and stir together.

Leave to cool before serving a portion to your dog. The remainder will keep in the fridge for up to 4 days.

· · · · · · · · · · · · · ❀ · · · · · · · · · · · · ·

Kcals/100 g (4 oz): 640
Protein: 30%
Fat: 12%

Top Tip

Baking the pumpkin rather than boiling it retains more of the nutrients.

Tuna and Sardine Fish Balls

Tuna is really good for the joints and internal organs, especially the heart, as well as giving dogs a lovely coat. Sardines are also very high in omega-3, vitamin D and selenium. I have also added ground flaxseed to this recipe for an extra omega-3 boost.

·············· ❀ ··············

1 x 130 g tin of tuna in sunflower oil
1 x 100 g tin of sardines in oil
200 g (7 oz) potatoes
100 g (4 oz) fresh spinach, or 50 g (2 oz) frozen spinach
1 tbsp ground flaxseed
1 tbsp chopped parsley

·············· ❀ ··············

Open the tins of tuna and sardines and pour the entire contents into a large bowl. Check for any large, hard bones in the sardines and discard. Mash the fish together and set aside.

Peel and roughly chop the potatoes, put in a pan of boiling water and cook for 15 minutes. Add the spinach to the potatoes for the last 5 minutes of cooking time.

Drain the potatoes and spinach and mash using a potato masher or fork. Add this vegetable mash to the fish, along with the ground flaxseed and parsley, and mix together.

Once the mixture is cool enough to handle, form it into about 6 balls, using your hands or 2 wooden spoons, and place on a plate. (Two of these balls will be enough for a meal for a small-to medium-sized dog.)

· · · · · · · · · · · · · ❀ · · · · · · · · · · · · ·

Kcals/100 g (4 oz): 340
Protein: 33%
Fat: 20%

· Top Tip ·

These fish balls will keep in the fridge for 5 days, but why not double up the recipe and freeze some (for up to 3 months)? You can then take them out as you need them and either leave them overnight in the fridge to defrost or pop them into the oven for 20 minutes. Leave them to cool before feeding to your dog.

Tasty Treats

Giving dogs a treat is a lovely way of acknowledging them for something they have done. These treats are all delicious, easy to make, and as different from the shop-bought ready-made 'treats' as you can imagine. Unfortunately, most of the mass-produced treats – and this includes the so-called 'natural' ones – are far from the description on the pack.

The worst culprits are those that are termed 'semi-moist', which need to have very strong preservatives added to stop them from becoming mouldy inside the pack. To give you an idea, this is the list of ingredients, not included on the label, that goes into any semi-moist treat: phosphoric acid, artificial anti-oxidants – propyl gallate, BHA (banned in the US), citric acid and a mould inhibitor – potassium sorbate. Not very natural!

The other things to watch out for in shop-bought treats are the levels of fat and sugar. Dogs adore both but it can be easy for them to pile on the pounds if you are feeding lots of very high-fat treats, and lots of sugary ones are obviously not great for their teeth either.

The best treats or snacks you can give your dog are those made in your own kitchen – and that way you know exactly what's gone into the recipe, too! These treats are suitable both for puppies, for whom you'll need treats at the ready for training, and for older dogs, who will appreciate a tasty tidbit of something delicious during the day.

Spelt and Sunflower Treats

These are good chunky treats for taking on walks. They won't crumble in your pocket and they are also really healthy, with lots of good oils. Spelt flour is a good alternative to wheat if your dog is intolerant to wheat, as although it is a form of wheat, it is a variety that dogs are unlikely to have built up an intolerance to.

················ ❀ ···············

50 g (2 oz) sunflower seeds
200 g (7 oz) spelt flour
1 tablespoon ground flaxseed
5 tbsp olive oil
½ tsp finely chopped fresh parsley
½ tsp finely chopped fresh rosemary
150 ml (¼ pint) water or milk

················ ❀ ···············

Preheat the oven to 180°C (350°C/gas 4). Lightly grease a baking sheet.

Roughly chop the sunflower seeds using either a knife or a pestle and mortar. Put into a bowl with all the other ingredients and mix together.

Take a small amount of the dough, roll into a ball the size of a golf ball and place onto the prepared baking sheet. When your baking sheet is full of small balls, press your thumb into the middle of each one to flatten slightly. Bake for 30 minutes until cooked through.

Transfer the treats from the oven onto a cooling rack and allow to cool. They can then be kept in a sealed container for up to a week.

················ ❀ ···············

Kcal/100 g (4 oz): 560
Protein: 11%
Fat: 30%

Oatmeal Biscuits

I love biscuit recipes that have no wheat flour in. Oats are low GI and a very good source of soluble protein and fibre for your dog. Oatmeal is just crushed oats, milled to different sizes. You can use either fine or medium here. Fine oatmeal is a bit easier to handle and less crumbly, but medium will be good too.

. . . . ❁ . . . .

225 g (8 oz) fine oatmeal
1 tbsp oil or fat, such as goose fat or beef dripping

. . . . ❁ . . . .

Preheat the oven to 180°C (350°C/gas 4). Lightly grease a baking sheet.

Measure out the oatmeal and place in a bowl, make a well in the centre to pour the liquid into.

Put the tablespoon of oil into the bowl. If you are using a hard fat, such as goose, then spoon this into the bowl and pour over 3 tablespoons of boiling water to melt the fat. Stir with a knife or spoon and it will quickly form a dough.

Lightly dust a clean work surface with some of the oatmeal and turn the dough out onto it. You can either roll out the dough to around 1 cm (½ in) thickness or just flatten it into shape with your hands.

Cut into pieces or use a small cookie cutter to cut into discs, place on the baking sheet and bake for about 20 minutes.

These biscuits will keep for up to 2 weeks in an airtight tin.

. . . . ❁ . . . .

Kcal/100 g (4 oz): 340
Protein: 9%
Fat: 14%

Variations

Mix one of the following to the oatmeal
before adding the oil or fat:
1 tbsp chopped fresh parsley
1 tbsp grated cheese
1 tsp blackstrap molasses
1 tsp finely chopped dried apple

Peanut Butter and Buckwheat Kisses

Buckwheat flour is a relative newcomer in the 'alternative' flour stakes. Despite having the word 'wheat' in it, it is in fact gluten free and has a lovely sweet, nutty taste. Peanut butter is a palatable fat to add if you have a finicky dog and want an alternative to animal fat. It also has a good level of protein.

· · · · · · · · · · · · · 🐾 · · · · · · · · · · · · ·

200 g (7 oz) buckwheat flour
50 g (2 oz) porridge oats
1 tsp blackstrap molasses
100 g (4 oz) smooth peanut butter

· · · · · · · · · · · · · 🐾 · · · · · · · · · · · · ·

Preheat the oven to 180°C (350°C/gas 4). Lightly grease a baking sheet.

Put the flour and oats into a bowl.

Measure the blackstrap molasses out into a small bowl, pour over 100 ml (4 fl oz) boiling water and stir until dissolved. Add in the peanut butter and stir. Add to the rest of the ingredients in the bowl and mix together to form a nice soft dough. (If it is a little dry, then add a few tablespoons of water.)

Lightly flour a clean work surface and turn out the dough onto it. Taking small pieces of the dough, roll them into small balls – about half the size of a golf ball. Put them on the prepared baking sheet and press down gently on each ball with your thumb. Bake in the oven for 25 minutes.

Leave the biscuits to cool (they should be quite hard), then store in a sealed container. They should keep for at least a week.

· · · · · · · · · · · · · 🐾 · · · · · · · · · · · · ·

Kcals/100 g (4 oz): 400
Protein: 13%
Fat: 30%

Cheesy Breakfast Bars

These are a great addition to your pet's pantry. They are handy to take on a long journey if there hasn't been time for breakfast (or supper) and you know you aren't going to be able to scoop out some food for your dog. They are also good as a big treat if you're on a long walk and suppertime seems like a long way off.

This recipe makes about eight bars. Lily, who weighs 12 kg (26 lb), will have two of them as an emergency meal replacement, or one as a big treat.

················⊛················

200 g (7 oz) rolled oats
2 tbsp honey
50 g (2 oz) Cheddar cheese, grated
3 tbsp sunflower oil
25 g (1 oz) fresh parsley or rosemary, finely chopped
1 egg, beaten

················⊛················

Preheat the oven to 180°C (350°C/gas 4). Lightly grease a baking tin.

Put all the ingredients into a saucepan. Stir over a low heat for a couple of minutes and then pour into the baking tin.

Smooth down the mixture firmly using the back of a wooden spoon. Bake in the oven for 20 minutes until golden brown.

Remove from the oven and leave to cool slightly before cutting into 8 equal bars. Leave to cool completely in the tin. The bars will keep in an airtight container for 10 days in the fridge.

················⊛················

Kcals/100 g (4 oz): 420
Protein: 10%
Fat: 16%

Cheesy Twists

These are fun to make and you can keep them for ten days in a sealed jar. They have a small amount of cheese in, which dogs love, as well as some flaxseed for an omega-3 boost. However, because they are high in fat, you should limit your dog to a couple a day.

Flour, for dusting
200 g (7 oz) puff pastry
50 g (2 oz) Cheddar cheese, grated
50 g (2 oz) ground flaxseed

Preheat the oven to 180°C (350°C/gas 4). Lightly grease a baking sheet.

On a lightly floured work surface, roll out the puff pastry into a rough square shape about 1 cm (½ in) thick. Scatter the grated cheese over the surface, then sprinkle over the ground flaxseed. Press these toppings into the pastry firmly with your hand.

Cut the pastry into long strips, then cut the strips in half so you have lots of 3 cm (1¼ in) pieces. Take each strip and twist it. (If you prefer, you can cut the pastry into disc shapes with a small cookie cutter instead.)

Place on a lightly greased baking sheet and put in a medium oven for 20 minutes.

Let them cool completely and then store in an airtight container.

Kcals/100 g (4 oz): 500
Protein: 12%
Fat: 30%

Fishy Treats

Some dogs go crazy for fish and this is a good way of getting them to eat a really healthy snack that they will adore. You can feed up to two or three of these a day. They are also fun and very easy to make.

················ ✿ ················

1 x 200 g tin of tuna or salmon in oil
1 egg, beaten
100 g (4 oz) flour

················ ✿ ················

Preheat the oven to 180°C (350°C/gas 4). Lightly grease a baking sheet.

Empty the fish and its oil into a bowl and flake with a fork. Add the beaten egg and stir well to combine.

Add the flour and mix together so that you have a lumpy dough. You can either roll out the dough and cut up into small squares, or pick up small pieces of dough and roll into little balls.

Place the shapes on the baking sheet and bake in the oven for 20 minutes until golden brown and cooked through.

Once they are cooled, you can store them in a container in the fridge for up to 2 weeks.

················ ✿ ················

Kcals/100 g (4 oz): 380
Protein: 38%
Fat: 13%

Mini Meaty Balls

These delicious training treats smell very appetizing. Offer one to your disappearing dog and he will be sure to come racing back to you! Don't feed too many though as they are very high in calories!

· · · · · · · · · · · · · · ❀ · · · · · · · · · · · · · ·

300 g minced lamb or turkey
I egg
50 g (2 oz) brown rice flour
I tsp parsley

· · · · · · · · · · · · · · ❀ · · · · · · · · · · · · · ·

Put all the ingredients into a food processor and blend until you have a nice soft consistency like bread dough.

Roll the mixture into small, marble-sized balls and place on a lightly greased baking sheet. Put them in the fridge for an hour so they really hold their shape when they are cooked. Meanwhile, heat the oven to 180°C (350°F/gas 4).

Place the meaty balls in the oven and cook for 45 minutes. They should be hard rather than crumbly. If you have used lamb then drain off the fat.

· · · · · · · · · · · · · · ❀ · · · · · · · · · · · · · ·

Kcals/100 g (4 oz): 780
Protein: 42%
Fat: 18%

· Table Scraps ·

We sometimes don't think twice about feeding our dog the 'leftovers' after a meal. But you do need to make sure that you are not feeding scraps that are salty or peppery. Giving a dog some gravy seems like a lovely idea, but do bear in mind that the gravy will have been seasoned for humans and not for dogs, so it's likely to be far too salty.

The other thing to avoid is feeding table scraps that are too fatty, for example the skin of a chicken you've cooked for the family. Doing so could cause a bout of pancreatitis if your dog is sensitive to fat.

Fresh produce

Power Treats

These small liver cake treats are designed for dogs who often turn their nose up at treats. I defy a dog to refuse these ones! They are bursting with really great ingredients, each of which has a specific nutritional purpose. This recipe has a two-stage cooking process to make sure the treats are properly cooked through.

. . . . ·❀· . . . .

2 eggs
250 g (8 oz) fresh liver, roughly chopped
50 g (2 oz) Cheddar cheese, grated
½ tsp blackstrap molasses
300 g (11 oz) buckwheat or spelt flour

. . . . ·❀· . . . .

Preheat the oven to 180°C (350°C/gas 4). Lightly grease a baking sheet.

Break the eggs into the bowl of a food processor and add the liver, grated cheese and blackstrap molasses. Blitz to purée together.

Add in the flour and blitz to combine. You should now have a nice soft dough. The dough will be quite sticky so it's a good idea to put plenty of flour on your hands to handle it.

Take out the dough and put it straight onto the prepared baking sheet. Flatten it down with your hands so that it is about 1 cm (½ in) thick. Alternatively, roll the dough into a cylinder on a lightly floured surface and chop it into disc shapes. Bake for about 20 minutes.

Remove from the oven and cut up the dough into small squares; tiny size if you have a small dog and larger if your dog is bigger – you know what size treat your dog is used to!

Reduce the oven temperature to 150°C (300°F/gas 2). Put the shapes back into the oven and leave to dry out completely for 2 hours.

Remove them from the oven and leave to cool completely before storing them in an airtight container in the fridge for up to 2 weeks.

· · · · · · · · · · · · · · · · ✿ · · · · · · · · · · · · · · · ·

Kcals/100 g (4 oz): 390
Protein: 30%
Fat: 14%

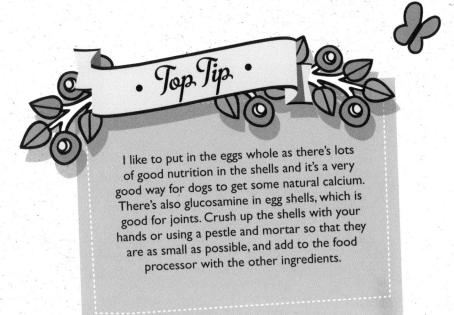

• Top Tip •

I like to put in the eggs whole as there's lots of good nutrition in the shells and it's a very good way for dogs to get some natural calcium. There's also glucosamine in egg shells, which is good for joints. Crush up the shells with your hands or using a pestle and mortar so that they are as small as possible, and add to the food processor with the other ingredients.

Pure Liver Treats

There are moments when you need a piece of something very tasty to coax your dog away from a rabbit (or a fox, in Lily's case). These treats are very easy to make and you can make them plain and simple or sprinkle them with a teaspoon of dried alfalfa, aniseed, parsley or garlic powder before you put them into the oven.

· · · · · · · · · · · · · ❀ · · · · · · · · · · · · · ·

200 g (7 oz) chicken livers

· · · · · · · · · · · · · ❀ · · · · · · · · · · · · · ·

Preheat the oven to 180°C (350°C/gas 4). Line a baking tin with greaseproof paper.

Pop the livers into a saucepan of boiling water for 5 minutes. This makes them much easier to slice. (You can just chop them without boiling them, but they are rather slithery.)

Once they are roughly chopped, put them into the prepared baking tin and place in the oven for 45 mins–1 hour. You need the livers to be nicely dried out so they will keep well.

Once the liver pieces are dried out, remove them from the oven and let them cool in the tray. You can keep them in an airtight container in the fridge for 2 weeks or freeze them for up to 2 months.

· · · · · · · · · · · · · ❀ · · · · · · · · · · · · · ·

Kcals/100 g (4 oz): 425
Protein: 60%
Fat: 20%

Dried Apple Rings

Another simple treat recipe that is very healthy for your dog and virtually fat free! Lily loves apples in all varieties and this is a good low-fat treat you can feed without worrying about putting weight on your dog. Dogs love anything sweet, so these treats make a nice change from the savoury treats they usually get.

· · · · · · · · · · · · · ⊗ · · · · · · · · · · · · ·

Apples – any variety but check they are not bruised

· · · · · · · · · · · · · 🐾 · · · · · · · · · · · · ·

Preheat the oven to 160°C (325°F/gas 3).

Peel and core the apples and slice into rings. Place the rings on a baking sheet and put into the oven to bake for about 6 hours.

They should be dry and 'leathery' when they are done, rather than crispy (although crispy is also fine). The more moisture you take out of them, the longer they will keep. They will keep for 2–4 weeks in an airtight container depending on how dry they are.

· · · · · · · · · · · · · ⊗ · · · · · · · · · · · · ·

Kcals/100 g (4 oz): 58
Protein: 1%
Fat: 0%

Top Tip

You can cook the apples faster on a higher heat but you will need to keep an eye on them as they do tend to burn quickly.

Fruity Granola Squares

Dogs love fruit and one of Lily's favourites is apples, which is why I like to include them in lots of recipes. They are a good source of vitamin C and fibre and also provide sweetness, which dogs like. Blackstrap molasses is a great source of B vitamins and iron.

· · · · · · · · · · · · · · · ❁ · · · · · · · · · · · · · ·

50 g (2 oz) sunflower seeds
200 g (7 oz) oats
100 g (4 oz) apple purée (see tip)
3 tbsp sunflower oil
1 tbsp blackstrap molasses
1 tbsp dried, ground rosehips

· · · · · · · · · · · · · · · ❁ · · · · · · · · · · · · · ·

Preheat the oven to 180°C (350°C/gas 4). Lightly grease a baking tin.

Grind the sunflower seeds in a food processor, or crush them using a pestle and mortar until they are roughly ground (this is so your dog can make good use of the nutrition – if they are whole they will simply pass straight through and not be digested properly).

Pour the crushed sunflower seeds and the oats into a saucepan and stir to combine.

Put the apple purée, sunflower oil, blackstrap molasses and rosehips into a bowl and stir to combine.

Pour this mixture over the dry ingredients in the pan. Stir gently over a medium heat until the molasses has melted and then transfer to the baking tin. Smooth down the mixture firmly using the back of a wooden spoon and transfer the tin to the oven to bake for 20 minutes until golden brown.

Remove from the oven and allow to cool slightly, then cut up into squares or rectangles. Leave to cool completely in the tin. These will keep for a week in a sealed container.

· · · · · · · · · · · · · ❀ · · · · · · · · · · · · ·

Kcals/100 g (4 oz): 420
Protein: 8%
Fat: 17%

Top Tip

You can use a ready-made apple purée from a health food shop or a good-quality organic one from your supermarket. Alternatively, you can make your own: peel, core and chop 2 apples into small pieces and put into a saucepan with 50 ml (2 fl oz) water to prevent sticking. Simmer on a low heat for 10 minutes.

Treats for a Hot Day

There are lots of healthy treats you can make for your dog that will help them cool down when it's a sweltering day. Here are some simple ideas for frozen treats.

...............●...............

Peanut Butter Pops

Put 3 tablespoons of smooth peanut butter into a bowl and stir in 400 ml (14 fl oz) of water to loosen the consistency. Pour into an ice-cube tray and freeze.

Kcals/100 g (4 oz): 140
Protein: 11%
Fat: 18%

...............●...............

Apple Pops

In a measuring jug, mix equal quantities of apple juice and water. Pour into an ice-cube tray and freeze.

Kcals/100 g (4 oz): 30
Protein: 2%
Fat: 0%

- - - - - - - - - - - - · ✿ · - - - - - - - - - - - -

Frozen Fruity Treats

As a variation on the above recipe, pop blueberries, chopped
strawberries and/or raspberries into each section and freeze.

Kcals/100 g (4 oz): 30
Protein: 2%
Fat: 0%

- - - - - - - - - - - - · ✿ · - - - - - - - - - - - -

Frozen Banana Treats

Peel and then chop up a ripe banana. Put the slices on a plate or
baking tray and put into the freezer. Once frozen, transfer them to a
plastic bag and return to the freezer to use as and when required.

Kcals/100 g (4 oz): 95
Protein: 1%
Fat: 0%

Recovery Recipes

We get to know our dogs so well that we can tell the minute they are out of sorts. When Lily isn't feeling well, she loses her terrier-like independence and follows me everywhere. It's at times like these I wish she could talk and tell me exactly what she is feeling and where it hurts.

If your dog loses his or her appetite, it's always a good idea to visit the vet to see what's going on, in case it's something serious. It could, for example, be some sort of food intolerance or allergy. Just as many people are gluten-intolerant, so are a growing number of dogs. Gluten is a combination of two proteins found in many grains; wheat is the worse offender.

If you think your dog is off colour because of an allergy to something, then see if you can make the link between what they've been eating and any reaction this may have caused. Probably one of the most allergy-causing meats for dogs is chicken as derivatives of it are so widely used in dog foods. If you suspect this might be the case, you could try feeding fish, turkey or venison instead and cut out gluten until he or she is back to normal again.

Dogs love sweet things, so when your dog is not feeling too well and needs coaxing to eat something, it's great to include a variety of lovely sweet vegetables and fruit to help restore his or her appetite.

Pick-me-up Breakfast

If your dog needs a nutritious breakfast that will put the sparkle back, then this is a quick and easy recipe to make. There are no exotic ingredients in this recipe, but the ingredients here all provide a healthy and tasty pick-me-up for when your dog is feeling a bit low – perhaps after an operation. Eggs are an excellent source of protein and can be fed to your dog once or twice a week.

· · · · · · · · · · · · · ❀ · · · · · · · · · · · · ·

50 g (2 oz) oats
100 ml (4 fl oz) water or milk
1 tbsp vegetable oil
2 eggs, beaten
100 g (4 oz) cottage cheese
1 tsp dried (or 1 tbsp finely chopped fresh) herbs (see pages 122–3)

· · · · · · · · · · · · · ❀ · · · · · · · · · · · · ·

Soak the oats for 15 minutes in the water or milk.

Heat the oil in a frying pan, then add the beaten egg and scramble.

Once cooked, stir in the cottage cheese, soaked oats and herbs.

Allow to cool to room temperature before serving.

· · · · · · · · · · · · · ❀ · · · · · · · · · · · · ·

Kcals/100 g (4 oz): 320
Protein: 28%
Fat: 15%

Chicken and Barley Soup

The classic combination of chicken and pearl barley is the essence of a comforting, homemade meal. When I last made this, Lily and I shared the recipe! This soup also looks very pretty, with its lovely creamy orange colour.

Orange vegetables are great for dogs and according to a 2005 issue of the *Journal of the American Veterinary Medical Association*, dogs that consume orange or yellow vegetables at least three times a week are at a lower risk of developing cancer. It must be because these vegetables have a high level of beta-carotene, which will also help give your dog a beautiful coat.

· · · · · · · · · · · · · ❀ · · · · · · · · · · · · ·

Chicken carcase from a roast
2 garlic cloves, peeled
200 g (7 oz) carrots
2 apples
500 g (18 oz) sweet potatoes
100 g (3½ oz) pearl barley, rinsed under cold water
½ tsp ground flaxseed

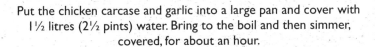

Put the chicken carcase and garlic into a large pan and cover with 1½ litres (2½ pints) water. Bring to the boil and then simmer, covered, for about an hour.

Meanwhile, prepare the vegetables: peel and roughly chop the carrots and apples making sure you remove the pips. Peel or scrub the sweet potatoes and chop roughly.

Remove the chicken pan from the heat and strain through a sieve and into a bowl. You will now have a delicious-smelling stock in the bowl and the leftover carcase in the sieve.

When the carcase is cool enough for you to handle it, pick off any bits of chicken that are left and set aside.

Put the strained liquid into a clean saucepan and add the pearl barley and prepared vegetables. Cover with the lid, bring to the boil and then simmer gently for about an hour.

Leave to cool, add in any pieces of chicken from the carcase and whizz the mixture in a food processor until smooth. It may seem a bit more like a purée than a soup, but that's fine and your dog will love it!

You can keep this soup in the fridge for up to 5 days or freeze it for up to 2 months. Serve with the ground flaxseed sprinkled on top.

Kcals/100 g (4 oz): 220
Protein: 28%
Fat: 1%

Top Tip

You could also add some homemade kibble pieces to this soup as 'croutons' (see pages 46–7).

Soothing Meals for Upset Tummies

If your dog has a bout of diarrhoea, you will need to feed something very bland that will settle him or her again. Diarrhoea can have all sorts of causes, but the most likely one is that your dog has eaten something he or she shouldn't have done while out on a walk or in the garden. If his or her stomach does not settle after a day or two, or if your dog is vomiting, you should contact your vet for advice. Here are a few ideas for suitable foods for dogs suffering with diarrhoea:

· · · · · · · · · · · · · ❀ · · · · · · · · · · · · ·

Chicken Pasta

100 g (4 oz) dried pasta
1 cube low-salt chicken stock cube

Cook the pasta according to the packet instructions, adding a low-salt chicken stock cube to the cooking water. Drain, cool to room temperature and then serve a small amount to your dog. You can keep any unused pasta in the fridge for up to 2 days.

Kcals/100 g (4 oz): 490
Protein: 11%
Fat: 2%

Top Tip

If your dog is better the next day then you can cook up some mince — something low in fat like chicken or turkey and mix this, with the remaining pasta.

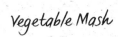

Vegetable Mash

200 g (7 oz) potatoes, peeled and diced
200 g (7 oz) carrots, peeled and diced

Add the diced vegetables to a pan of boiling water and cook for
15 minutes. Drain then mash together. Allow to cool to room
temperature and then serve a small amount to your dog.

Kcals/100 g (4 oz): 290
Protein: 7%
Fat: 0%

Calming Oats

Oats are said to build and strengthen, and they are ideal if you have a
dog that needs a calming, soothing meal.

100 g (4 oz) oats

Put the oats into a pan with 600 ml (1 pint) water and cook for
10 minutes. Leave to cool completely in the pan. A bit of patience
is needed here as it will take an hour or so for the mixture to cool
down enough for your dog to be able to eat it without being scalded.

Kcals/100 g (4 oz): 380
Protein: 9%
Fat: 5%

Stew for Sad Dogs

On days when your dog seems under the weather and in need of some TLC, this warming, heartening stew with its lovely selection of sweet vegetables and fruit will help get his or her tail wagging again.

500 g (1 lb 2 oz) turkey meat (e.g. breast or thighs) or mince
1 tbsp vegetable oil
3 or 4 parsnips, peeled and diced
6 large carrots, peeled or scrubbed and diced
200 g (7 oz) oats
2 sweet eating apples
2 tbsp runny honey
1 tsp dried (or 1 tbsp finely chopped fresh) herbs (see pages 122–3)
1 tsp ground flaxseed

Dice or chop the turkey meat, making sure there are no bones. Heat the oil in a saucepan, add the meat and brown over a medium heat. If you are using mince then just loosen this slightly and put it in the pan.

Add the parsnips, carrots, oats and about 300 ml (10 fl oz) of water (enough to cover all the ingredients). Bring to the boil, then reduce the heat, cover and simmer for about 20 minutes.

Once the stew has cooked, peel, core and grate the apple and stir it into the stew along with the honey, herbs and ground flaxseed.

Feed to your dog once it is cool enough to eat. If it's a cold day, you can serve it warm, but not hot. It will keep in the fridge for 4 days.

Kcals/100 g (4 oz): 350
Protein: 19%
Fat: 8%

Quick Doggy Ice Cream

Lily adores the taste of yoghurt! Yoghurt is, of course, full of lots of good bacteria that are good for your dog's stomach and will help him or her digest food well. This is a good recipe to make if your dog is on a course of antibiotics.

---

150 ml (¼ pint) natural yoghurt
50 g (2 oz) blueberries

In a small bowl, stir together the natural yoghurt and blueberries. You can either keep the blueberries whole or mash them in with the yoghurt.

Pour into an ice-cube tray and freeze. Once frozen you can pop a couple of cubes out to feed to your dog.

Kcals/100 g (4 oz): 60
Protein: 4%
Fat: 1%

Old Hounds

I don't think there's a fixed age when dogs become 'old hounds'. However, you will probably notice your dog getting a bit slower and more prone to hanging around in his or her basket for longer periods. Old dogs are also likely to get a bit stiffer in their joints and may become slightly more cantankerous and lose interest in performing their usual tricks.

When it becomes clear that your dog has reached his or her dotage (usually from about eight years old onwards depending on breed and level of activity), you will probably need to reduce the amount of food by about 20 per cent. Older dogs won't run around as much as younger ones so they need fewer calories if they are to avoid piling on the pounds.

It's important to make sure your older dog has good mental stimulation and gets at least 20 minutes of exercise every day. You can definitely teach an old dog new tricks and it's a great way to keep him or her happy and stimulated!

You'll also need to keep an eye out for any joint issues or possible hereditary health issues. There is a range of holistic remedies with which you can treat your dog if he or she does develop joint problems, and there are plenty of holistic and homeopathic vets who will be able to help you with choosing the right treatment.

The recipes in this book are all suitable for older dogs, but the ones in this chapter are especially good as they have lots of extra nutritional benefits and are particularly delicious, to tempt older dogs that may have lost their appetite.

Salmon Bake

Salmon is a fantastic fish, rich in nutrients. It contains lots of omega-3s, which are good for overall health and will benefit your dog's coat, skin, joints and internal organs. Salmon also aids brain development, and some studies have shown that it can also ward off arthritis.

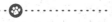

300 g (11 oz) sweet potatoes, peeled or scrubbed and chopped
100 g (4 oz) oats
200 g tin of salmon in sunflower oil
200 g (7 oz) carrots, peeled and grated
2 apples, peeled, cored and grated
100 g (4 oz) natural yoghurt
1 egg, beaten
1 tbsp ground flaxseed

Preheat the oven to 180°C (350°F/gas 4). Put the sweet potato into a pan and cover with water. Bring to the boil, reduce the heat and simmer for 15 minutes until cooked, then drain and mash roughly.

Meanwhile, put the oats in a pan with 400 ml (14 fl oz) of water and cook for 10 minutes.

Pour the contents of the tin of salmon into a large bowl and mash. Add the mashed sweet potatoes, cooked oats, grated carrot and apple, yoghurt and beaten egg. Mix together well. Spoon the mixture into an ovenproof dish and bake in the oven for 40 minutes.

Remove from the oven and sprinkle the top with the ground flaxseed. Allow to cool before serving. This will keep up to 4 days in the fridge.

Kcals/100 g (4 oz): 350
Protein: 18%
Fat: 9%

Comforting Chicken Stew

Older dogs tend to have a lower metabolism and need less food than they did when younger. They often become more picky about what they eat, so feeding them something delicious as well as nutritious is crucial. I firmly believe that you can help make sure your dog has a long and healthy life through a really good diet. It's important to keep the immune system as strong as possible by feeding plenty of vegetables, fruits and good-quality proteins. And keep him or her away from preservative-laden 'treats' and 'chews'!

············•❀•············

200 g (7 oz) potatoes, peeled and chopped into small pieces
100 g (4 oz) carrots, peeled and chopped into small pieces
100 g (4 oz) broccoli
500g (1 lb 2 oz) chicken thighs
100 g (4 oz) liver
50 g (2 oz) blueberries
1 tsp flaxseed oil
½ tsp ground rosehips
½ tsp ground flaxseed

Put the potatoes and carrots into a pan of water, bring to the boil, then reduce the heat, cover and simmer for 15 minutes. Add the broccoli to the saucepan for the last 5 minutes of cooking time.

Put the chicken and liver in a pan and cover with water. Bring to the boil, then reduce the heat, cover and simmer gently for 15–20 minutes until the chicken is cooked.

Drain the chicken and livers and chop into small pieces, removing and discarding any chicken bones. Place in a large mixing bowl.

Drain the vegetables and add to the chopped meat along with the blueberries, flaxseed oil, ground rosehips and ground flaxseed. Stir well to mix together.

Spoon out enough for your dog's meal, then cover the remainder and store in the fridge for up to 4 days.

Kcals/100 g (4 oz): 450
Protein: 32%
Fat: 30%

Wholesome Hash

Turmeric is commonly used for older dogs as it helps with the joints and circulation and is also anti-inflammatory. It's also good to include plenty of good oils in your dog's diet at this stage to help with lubricating the joints as well as for a shiny coat and overall health.

· · · · · · · · · · · · · · ❁ · · · · · · · · · · · · · ·

150 g (5 oz) brown rice
50 g (2 oz) porridge oats
400 g (14 oz) beef mince
200 g (7 oz) green leafy vegetable, e.g. cabbage or spinach, shredded
100 g (4 oz) apples
50 g (2 oz) ground flaxseed
1 tbsp salmon oil
1 tsp dried (or 1 tbsp finely chopped fresh) herbs (see pages 122–3)
1 tsp turmeric

· · · · · · · · · · · · · · ❁ · · · · · · · · · · · · · ·

Put the rice into a sieve and rinse under running water, then tip it into a saucepan. Cover with 700 ml (1¼ pints) of water, bring to the boil, then reduce the heat, cover and simmer for about 15 minutes until cooked. Stir in the porridge oats and leave for 5 minutes.

Meanwhile, brown the beef mince gently in a frying pan for about 15 minutes until cooked through. Cook the spinach or cabbage in a little water until softened.

Peel, core and grate the apples and place in a large bowl. Add the cooked rice and oats, mince and greens and all other remaining ingredients and mix thoroughly.

Serve a portion to your dog and store the remainder, covered, in the fridge for up to 4 days.

· · · · · · · · · · · · · · ❁ · · · · · · · · · · · · · ·

Kcals/100 g (4 oz): 580
Protein: 24%
Fat: 20%

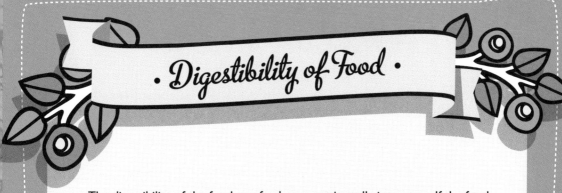

· Digestibility of Food ·

The digestibility of the food you feed your pet is really important. If the food is properly digested it means that your pet will be making really good use of all the nutrition available in the ingredients and just pooping out what he or she doesn't need. If you feed a good food, there's less waste!

When nutrients are properly absorbed in the small intestine, the remainder of the bowel is allowed to rest and there will be few undigested nutrients that go on to the large intestine.

If your dog has a particularly hard time digesting food and it seems that everything you feed just goes straight through, then do try some of the wholesome recipes in this book. Choose the ones that have a single source of protein, e.g. just lamb or chicken or turkey, together with a gluten-free carbohydrate like rice, lentils or potato.

Dogs just love real food made from fresh ingredients

Winter Hotpot

A nice warming meal that will give your old hound a healthy, nutritious boost. I've chosen some winter favourites here – oats and pearl barley, which are both low GI and will therefore help your dog feel fuller for longer, together with some seasonal vegetables. The vegetables provide a rainbow of colours to maximize nutrition and help boost immunity. The herbs used here – rosehips, parsley and garlic – all have healing properties and are full of antioxidants for optimum health.

· · · · · · · · · · · · · 🐾 · · · · · · · · · · · · ·

150 g (5 oz) pearl barley
1 garlic clove, peeled and sliced
500 g (1 lb 2 oz) potatoes, peeled and roughly chopped
100 g (4 oz) carrots, peeled and roughly chopped
50 g (2 oz) green beans, chopped
100 g (4 oz) broccoli (4 or 5 florets), chopped
500 g (1 lb 2 oz) minced lamb or turkey or beef
1 tbsp vegetable oil (optional, see method)
100 g (4 oz) oats
½ tsp ground rosehips
1 tsp finely chopped fresh parsley

· · · · · · · · · · · · · 🐾 · · · · · · · · · · · · ·

Put the pearl barley in a pan with the garlic and cover with 700 ml (1¼ pints) of water. Bring to the boil, then reduce the heat, cover and simmer for about 40 minutes until the pearl barley is soft.

Put the potatoes, carrots and green beans into a pan and cover with water. Bring to the boil, then reduce the heat and simmer for about 20 minutes until all the vegetables are soft. Add the broccoli to the pan for the last 5 minutes of cooking time.

Meanwhile, brown the mince in a frying pan over a medium to high heat for about 10 minutes until it is thoroughly cooked. If you are using turkey, which is a very lean meat, add a tablespoon of oil to the pan before cooking to prevent sticking.

Once the vegetables are cooked, remove the pan from the heat and stir in the oats. Leave for 5 minutes then add the cooked meat, cooked pearl barley, ground rosehips and chopped parsley. Stir the whole mixture, breaking up any lumpy vegetables and leave to cool.

This will keep in the fridge for 4 days.

Kcals/100 g (4 oz): 500
Protein: 20%
Fat: 12%

• Top Tip •

I recommend chopping the green beans as finely as you can; otherwise, if your dog is anything like Lily, they will be neatly left in the bowl at the end of the meal. If I chop them up into small pieces, Lily doesn't notice them and will just eat them up with everything else.

Supergrain Medley

This is a great recipe to which to add meat, for example the leftovers from a Sunday joint, and some vegetables to make a balanced meal. These supergrains should make up around 30 per cent of the dish.

· · · · · · · · · · · · · ❂ · · · · · · · · · · · · ·

100 g (4 oz) brown rice
100 g (4 oz) quinoa
100 g (4 oz) pearled barley

· · · · · · · · · · · · · ❂ · · · · · · · · · · · · ·

Put all the grains into a sieve and rinse under cold running water. If you have time, soak them overnight (this will retain more of their nutrition and they will also cook more quickly).

Put the grains into a saucepan and pour over 1 litre (1¾ pints) water. Bring to the boil, then reduce the heat, cover and simmer for about 30 minutes until they are soft.

Uncover and leave to cool before feeding to your dog. Store, covered, in the fridge for up to a week.

· · · · · · · · · · · · · ❂ · · · · · · · · · · · · ·

Kcals/100 g (4 oz): 360
Protein: 10%
Fat: 4%

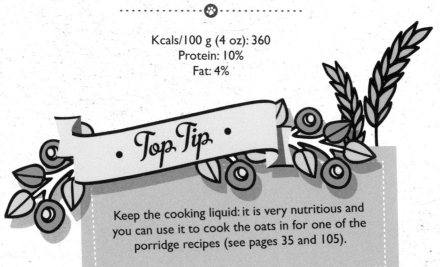

Top Tip

Keep the cooking liquid: it is very nutritious and you can use it to cook the oats in for one of the porridge recipes (see pages 35 and 105).

Carrot Cakes

These treats are bursting with carroty goodness. Lily loves carrots and I put this recipe together as it's good for her to occasionally have a non-meaty treat that's also very satisfying. These carrot cakes have a comforting taste and aroma and if you are feeding them to your older dog, they will also give him or her a little energy burst thanks to their natural sweetness.

· · · · · · · · · · · · · 🐾 · · · · · · · · · · · · ·

150g (5 oz)/2 carrots, peeled and grated
50 g (2 oz) oats
100 ml (4 fl oz) milk
100 g (4 oz) brown rice flour
1 tsp molasses
100 g (4 oz) apple purée
1 tbsp vegetable oil
50 g (2 oz) blueberries (optional)

· · · · · · · · · · · · · 🐾 · · · · · · · · · · · · ·

Preheat the oven to 180°C (350°C/gas 4). Lightly grease a baking sheet.

Put all of the ingredients into a mixing bowl and mix together thoroughly.

Drop spoonfuls of the mixture onto the prepared baking tray and bake for 30 minutes.

These cakes will keep for up to a week in a sealed container.

· · · · · · · · · · · · · 🐾 · · · · · · · · · · · · ·

Kcals/100 g (4 oz): 350
Protein: 7%
Fat: 10%

One of the best things about cooking for your dog is that you can tailor the meals to provide what your dog needs at the time and add in some healthy extras, such as herbs and certain spices. (Herbs are the leaves of the plant and spices are from the roots, flowers, seeds, bark or berries of the plant.)

Dogs have evolved to eat herbs in nature over the centuries and indeed I often hear of dogs chewing on rosemary bushes or eating mint from the garden. There's something that feels very naturally nutritious about including herbs in your dog's food.

It's worth remembering that our most commonly used medicines have their origins in the herbs and plants of the natural world.

There are some herbs that I like to use regularly. You're unlikely to grow many of them in your garden, but if you search online you will find several good companies that can supply these herbs to you. Ideally, use organic or wild-crafted herbs, which grow native to their habitat and have had as little interference as possible and not been exposed to pollutants, pesticides or artificial fertilizers. If you are able to use fresh herbs – for example mint, parsley, rosemary or thyme – so much the better. As a general guideline, 1 teaspoon of dried is the equivalent of 1 tablespoon of finely chopped fresh herbs. (If you're using ground herbs, you can safely use the same quantity as for dried.)

All the herbs listed here are safe to use at home in moderation. You can buy them in dried or powder form and then mix them together to make your own superfood formulation. Add half a teaspoon per day to your dog's home-cooked meal.

If your dog has a specific medical condition that needs treating, then you should consult a vet who specializes in herbal treatments so that you can be sure your dog is getting the right dosage to help the specific condition that needs treating. If your dog is pregnant, you will need to check whether the herbs you want to use are suitable.

Here is a list of some of my favourite herbs to keep in your cupboard that are safe to use for your dog. You can put a tablespoon of each in a jar and mix them together. Then add in the required amount of your 'superherb' mixture to the recipe. Try to use dried herbs that are less than six months old so they still have their potency.

Alfalfa

A bit of a wonder herb as it contains a good variety of nutrients such as vitamin K, alfalfa is useful for when your dog is feeling a bit under the weather and is also very high in protein (up to 50 per cent). It is often recommended for joints and dogs with arthritis and is reputed to have anti-cancer properties and to help with mental agility, so is particularly good for older dogs. It is also known as a good treatment for bad breath.

Burdock root

A herb with lots of medicinal attributes, burdock root is used as a general tonic and is helpful in treating skin problems thanks to its antifungal properties. It is considered to be a blood cleanser and purifier and a tonic for the liver and kidneys.

Celery seeds

Good as a detoxifier and helpful therefore for treating bladder and urinary infections as well as arthritis, celery seeds are also known to have a calming effect on the digestive system and can be helpful to relieve gas.

Chamomile

Chamomile is well known for its calming effects, so helpful to relieve anxiety or to give to dogs that find it difficult to settle at night.

Chickweed

A soothing herb to help with digestion and stomach upsets, chickweed is also a traditional remedy for arthritis.

Cleavers

A traditional cleanser of the liver and detoxifier of the lymphatic system, cleavers is a rich source of vitamin C and helps soothe skin complaints.

Dandelion

A very gentle herb with many supportive and restorative benefits, dandelion is packed with many essential vitamins and minerals. The leaves are used as a diuretic and are good for the liver and digestive system, and the root, too, can be used as a digestive and liver tonic.

Kelp

Rich in essential minerals such as iodine, kelp is a favourite with show dogs as it's known to help with maintaining a glossy, shiny coat and strong healthy teeth. It is usually easily available as a powder.

Marigold petals

A good cleansing herb for the organs and skin.

Milk thistle

A herb that is full of antioxidants and is used to detoxify the liver and help keep it healthy.

Mint

A beneficial herb for digestion and bloating, mint also helps to freshen breath.

Nettles

A particularly rich source of minerals and vitamins (especially iron), nettles are good as a blood purifier and are helpful with skin conditions and allergies. You can also pick your own young nettles – wearing gloves, of course! – cover with water and simmer for 10 minutes. When cool, add a few tablespoons of the liquid and cooked leaves to your dog's food as a good overall tonic.

Parsley

Parsley is a must-have in your herbal pharmacy: both leaves and stems are very nutritious and contain lots of vitamins, minerals and fibre. Try to use fresh parsley if you can.

Rosehips

One of my favourite herbs, rosehips are one of nature's richest natural sources of vitamin C, which helps strengthen the immune system to help keep your dog really healthy. Rosehips are available in ground form from a herbalist.

Rosemary

A helpful herb that aids digestion, rosemary is said to be good for the heart as well as being useful to help calm nervous or excitable dogs.

Thyme

Thyme can be used to help treat kennel cough and is good if your dog has sore gums as it has good antiseptic qualities.

Turmeric

This spice has anti-inflammatory properties and helps with blood cleansing. It is often given to dogs (and humans) to treat arthritis.

The Lily's Kitchen Story

My dog Lily was allergic to all the pet foods I bought for her; she came out in rashes and then developed itchy ears and skin. Her fur also never seemed to look healthy. I became obsessed with trying to get to the bottom of why her skin was in such bad condition. My brother, who is a vet, thought it could be related to her food.

So I started cooking for Lily, making her fresh meals every day to see if this would make a difference. Within a couple of weeks, her skin and ears had calmed down, and after another two weeks all her 'hot spots' had disappeared. She stopped looking like a faded old broom and her fur became healthy and shiny. She also lost that rather pungent 'doggy smell', which many owners put up with and eventually become immune to.

Although delighted with the results, however, I was horrified that the food I had been feeding her had been causing these problems. I couldn't believe how blindly I had chosen food for her, believing all the claims on the pack. I felt sure there must be other people like me; indeed, my brother told me that of the numerous pet owners coming into his surgery with their dogs and cats, many had pets with dietary issues.

I decided that something needed to be done about the problem. I wasn't especially keen on cooking for Lily every day; I really wanted something ready made that I could trust 100 per cent and know would be good for her. After all, she shows me such devotion and I felt that I had let her down by choosing the wrong food for her.

The next step was spending eighteen months talking to a wide range of vets, both conventional and homeopathic, nutritionists and pet food experts. With their help, I began to put together a list of perfect ingredients for pets, and we started Lily's Kitchen with three recipes. It then took another year to find commercial kitchens who wanted to work with us – most of them turned us down the moment they saw the kinds of ingredients we wanted to make our food with. After visiting more than thirty places, I found the ones that were perfect for us.

We launched in November 2008 and almost immediately had a very loyal following. Like me, many pet owners had struggled to find something really healthy to feed their pet. People could see this was real food – not 'chunk and jelly' that smelled revolting, or dry food you have to open at arms' length because of the overwhelming smell of rancid grease.

We are now a team of eleven people and we all feel very proud of what we do. It's a privilege to be in a position to make such a difference to animals' quality of life.

My days are really varied but my favourite part of my job is developing new products in our kitchen. I've always had an interest in nutrition and healthy eating and I'm always on the hunt for new ingredients. While I'm creating a new recipe, I tend to hone in on an exciting new ingredient that has a medicinal benefit and build my recipe around this. For example, we have just launched some wonderful new treats called 'Power Flowers'. I really loved the idea of using turmeric for dogs because this spice has a long list of healing properties and is said to be very good for joints. So I put this together with some other ingredients, such as blackstrap molasses, which is full of B vitamins and very good for the blood.

I love the fact that we've created recipes that are really healthy for cats and dogs and that are filled with really good things so our pets can enjoy healthy meals and healthy lives.

For more on the Lily's Kitchen range, visit www.lilyskitchen.co.uk.

Index

Acknowledgements

I'd like to acknowledge all the lovely people at Lily's Kitchen I'm lucky enough to work with. They have been very supportive while I have been 'under cover' writing this book!

I'd like to thank our in-house vet, Holly Mash, who is an inspirational vet and always looking for a holistic alternative to the conventional route to wellness for pets. She has been invaluable with all her knowledge of herbs and nutrition.

I'd also like to thank Jeanette Quainton, who is our specialist nutritionist and has helped me with the nutritional information for the book. She is endlessly patient when I ask for advice on all sorts of ingredients that are not usually used in standard pet foods and has helped make our formulations satisfying and nutritious.

Thanks to the team at Ebury Press who have been so excited and enthusiastic about publishing this book. Many thanks to Sarah Such, Sara Pearson and Anne McDowall, and to Petra Borner for creating the original illustration for the Lily's Kitchen foods. And thanks to Mad River for their tireless enthusiasm in designing this book.

Thank you to my family and friends, especially my brother Bob the Vet – it seems like only yesterday that I met up with you after your interview at the Royal Veterinary School! Thank you to my friends for their endless encouragement and enthusiasm.

I'd especially like to acknowledge my partner Kim for all her support and for creating the peace and space in order for me to write this book. And I'd like to thank my daughter Holly for always being enthusiastic and for the endless cups of tea she provided for me while I was busy writing.

Last but not least, a big thank you to Lily. Without her I wouldn't truly understand the meaning of unconditional love. Thank you too, Lily, for always being a keen taster of all my recipes!